"The boy who wants to be  girl
who tried to prove that Jesı the
life story of two people whc ıeir
lives was different from w ıry
have lived and worked thı ınt
years teaching in Britain, r , ...a, ɒɪazil,
Singapore…Their story is a fascinating whirl."

Revd Professor John Goldingay
Professor of Old Testament, Fuller Seminary

"I want to thank David and Rosemary for sharing their missionary
life stories in Africa, Asia, and globally. We can feel both the joy and
excitement at the opportunities and the disappointments of setbacks
in their journey. Yet, this couple persevere, trust God is at work, and
see humour in adverse situations. Their heart to equip and train God's
people for God's global mission runs through the whole book."

Revd Dr Patrick Fung
General Director, OMF International

"I like reading books by Out of the Box people – and David and
Rosemary are this kind of people. Books like this are urgently needed.
Some say mission as a career is old hat and we are all missionaries. That's
true but we need people like David and Rosemary as much as ever
before. Please read the book and let some of this reality impact you."

George Verwer
Founder, Operation Mobilisation

"The Harleys share their journey in mission with honesty, humility
and humour. David and Rosemary are a superb example of a couple
in ministry and disciples together in mission. This wonderful book
brings the reader into the joys, but also the dangers and frustrations
of cross-cultural life and ministry. There is much wisdom shared in
these pages, with insights on leadership, global mission and what it
means to make the message of the gospel intelligible and meaningful
to those across the street or across the world. I'll be encouraging every
applicant to OMF, and every mission partner serving with OMF, to
read *Together in Mission*. I warmly commend this book and its authors."

Dr Peter Rowan PhD
Co-National Director, OMF (UK)

"David and Rosemary's friendship and support, welcoming me into their London home and their teaching and mentoring at All Nations Christian College, has been life-transforming. Their cross-cultural adventures in the UK, Africa and Asia, and their impact on the lives and ministries of so many others are told with their characteristic warmth, candour and humour. Their rich insights and practical experiences as a family committed to living out the Great Commission are a joy to read and an invaluable guide to God's mission today."

Dr Richard Harvey
Senior Researcher, Jews for Jesus

"Here is the story of David and Rosemary Harley's adventures with the Lord they love, who led them step by step in faith and obedience in ways they simply never expected. Both called to teach God's Word, both with pastoral hearts and global eyes, together in changing locations and circumstances they experienced the Lord's gentle guidance over a lifetime of service. Their lives have touched a host of people in many countries and of many nationalities, with resultant ripples for the gospel far beyond themselves. Read this book. You will laugh and cry and be stirred to pray and to want to follow the Lord more closely. What better reason to read a book?"

Rose Dowsett
Vice-Chair of WEA Mission Commission

"Some great Christian leaders are considered so because of their prominent public ministries; others are considered great because of the profound influence they have in the growth of the kingdom of God. David and Rosemary Harley belong to the second category. This book, written in an engaging and winsome style, describes the lives and ministries of two influential missionary leaders. As you read, you will be inspired and instructed about what it means to live for Christ, serve him and give leadership to his people."

Dr Ajith Fernando
Teaching Director, Youth for Christ, Sri Lanka

DAVID & ROSEMARY HARLEY

Together
in
Mission

From All Nations
to All Nations

MONARCH
BOOKS

Published by **Monarch Books**
www.lionhudson.com

Part of the SPCK Group
SPCK, 36 Causton Street, London, SW1P 4ST

ISBN 978 1 80030 034 7
e-ISBN 978 1 80030 038 5

First edition 2022

Acknowledgments

Map on page 46 by Catherine Harley

Unless otherwise marked Scripture quotations are taken from the *Holy Bible, New International Version*, copyright © 1973, 1978, 1984 International Bible Society. Used by permission of Hodder & Stoughton, a member of the Hodder Headline Group. All rights reserved. "NIV" is a trademark of International Bible Society. UK trademark number 1448790.

Scripture quotations marked RSV are from The Revised Standard Version of the Bible copyright © 1346, 1952 and 1971 by the Division of Christian Education of the National Council of Churches in the USA. Used by permission. All rights reserved.

Scripture quotations marked NLT are taken from the *Holy Bible, New Living Translation*, copyright © 1996, 2004, 2007 by Tyndale House Foundation. Used by permission of Tyndale House Publishers, Inc., Carol Stream, Illinois 60188. All rights reserved.

A catalogue record for this book is available from the British Library

Produced on paper from sustainable sources

Printed and bound in the UK, January 2022, LH26

Contents

Foreword **6**

Preface **9**

List of Abbreviations **12**

Chapter 1 • Called to Mission **13**

Chapter 2 • Together in Mission **26**

Chapter 3 • On the Roof of Africa **40**

Chapter 4 • Tales of the Unexpected **54**

Chapter 5 • Good News for Jewish People **70**

Chapter 6 • To All Nations **84**

Chapter 7 • College Principal **103**

Chapter 8 • Encouraging Mission Training Globally **117**

Chapter 9 • Singapore and World Mission **132**

Chapter 10 • General Director of OMF International **145**

Chapter 11 • Re-tyred **162**

Chapter 12 • Model for Mission **174**

Endnotes **189**

Bibliography **191**

Foreword

Priscilla and Aquila: that's who this book reminds me of. For that was another married couple who were "together in mission", supporting the ministry of the Apostle Paul and equipping Apollos for his cross-cultural missionary sending. (Acts 18:24–28) They are always mentioned together and Priscilla is usually mentioned first, just as David repeatedly and self-deprecatingly underlines and praises Rosemary's gifting and qualifications as a teacher.

Now, most married Christians who are serving in mission will express their appreciation for the *support* of their spouses. But Rosemary and David are unusual as a couple, *both of whom* have complementary callings and gifts, and who have genuinely worked and served together, enabling, encouraging and facilitating each other's ministry, even occasionally to the point of insisting that the one will not serve without the other. So this is not just a remarkable life story; it is also a challenging model of what genuine "partnership in mission" can look like, in a marriage where both honour the originality and integrity of each other's calling to serve the Lord. It reminded me of a small calligraphy picture that hung above my parents' bed: "Each for Other: Both for God."

A second big impression as one reads on, is just how flexible and adaptable David and Rosemary have had to be in their long career in mission. Some of the changes of direction came unbidden and were unwelcome, and they honestly convey the struggles and initial disappointments of such times. But equally, they show how God proved his faithfulness at each step as they responded with obedience and trust. That reminded me of how the Apostle Paul had to cope with occasions when the Holy Spirit said, "No, not this way," and then he had to wait, shelve his plans, and receive fresh direction. The gospel came to Europe after one such season of uncertainty, and with a note of irony too, in that Paul hears "a man from Macedonia" asking for help, but when he gets there, the first person to respond to the gospel is a *woman* from Thyatira – the land he had just left!

When the Harleys left All Nations Christian College in 1993, after one major phase in their ministry, I had been on the teaching staff there for five years and was about to take over from David as principal. As you will read, they were moving into a ministry of international training for mission for others on several continents. So I sought to keep them humble by calling them just "a pair of old trainers". My point is, they have been wholly committed to the crucial importance of proper training for the challenges of cross-cultural mission. Their story illustrates in several places the disasters that can happen when untrained men and women, full of zeal but little knowledge, are let loose in cultures not their own. Training costs time and money, but one lesson that I hope this book will reinforce, is that training is essential and well worth the cost.

You will probably lose count of the number of countries David and Rosemary have visited – but the cumulative impact is a kaleidoscopic awareness of the global church in all its diversity. And mission mirrors that kaleidoscope. The old adage that mission was "from the West to the Rest" was never true anyway. Mission has been going in all directions ever since the New Testament. Middle Eastern missionary bishops established the church in Ethiopia, for example, at least a hundred years before Patrick took the gospel to Ireland, and Syrian Christians had reached China half a millennium before Europeans even knew about the Americas. Bishops from Herat and Kandahar, in Afghanistan, participated in Christian synods in the 5th century. Ask Rosemary. With her experience of teaching the history of Christian mission, she can multiply such examples.

So the contemporary global diversity of the Christian church is not, in principle, a new thing. What the long ministry of the Harleys illustrates, however, is the way in which mission, as one dimension of the global church's inter-relatedness, is truly multi-directional and polycentric. We in the West have so much that we need to learn and receive from our sisters and brothers in the churches of

7

the majority world. It's not so much "from the West to the Rest", as "How the West needs the Rest". Reciprocity and humility must be the mode of our relating across ethnic and cultural boundaries that are become ever more porous. I think the Apostle Paul would heartily agree with that too.

There are some very funny moments in this book, which did not surprise me at all since the Harleys have spiced their lifetime in mission with their delightful sense of humour. Rosemary's infectious laughter was part of the ambience of ANCC and lightened many a staff meeting, while David never lacked a good joke or the ability to see the funny side of even the most intractable problems of college life. Unselfconsciously, they cultivated an ethos among us staff members that, while we took our work and calling with utmost seriousness, we did not take ourselves or each other too seriously. Laughter and teasing among ourselves were refreshing and joyous, while deep prayer and tears for our world and care for our students were paramount.

They would probably agree with me that, next to good training, a robust sense of humour is among the most valuable things anyone serving in mission must have in order to survive and thrive. That is probably because, in the midst of the agonies of our world and the passionate self-sacrificial love of God for his whole creation, our human sense of humour reflects God's own.

After all, how else could he have chosen people like us?

Chris Wright
Global Ambassador and Ministry Director
Langham Partnership

Preface

*"Go and make disciples of all nations… teaching them
to obey everything I have commanded you. And surely
I am with you always, to the very end of the age."*

Matthew 28:19–20

When both Rosemary and I put our trust in Jesus as young people
and asked him to guide us in our lives, we soon found these final
words of Jesus in our Bibles. They showed us that Jesus wanted his
first followers to go into all the world, because he has not just come
for them but for people of every nation. As we discovered, he still
wants people of every nation to hear the good news of who he is
and what he has done for them. This is the story of how Rosemary
and I found the parts God wanted us to play in this plan – how he
strengthened us, guided us, and provided for us.

As Jesus was leaving his followers, he told them to wait for the Holy
Spirit, who would give them the power to be his witnesses, starting
in Jerusalem (Acts 1:8). At first, they witnessed in Jerusalem. Later
some went to Jewish communities in the surrounding area. Philip
went to the Samaritans, traditional enemies of the Jews, while Paul
and his companions travelled extensively across the Mediterranean
region. Each went where God sent them.

Although we are familiar with the names of some who were
witnesses for Jesus, we know there were many others, whose names
we do not know, but who were later scattered far and wide and
shared their new-found faith. Each played their part and, in each
generation, Christians are called to follow their example. We hope
and pray that our story will encourage others to be open to his
leading. When we met, we had both felt called to mission, to serve
God outside our own country, so then we felt God was calling us to
serve him together.

9

After we got married we worked in a church in London before going to work in rural Africa. We expected to work there until we retired. Little did we know that our lives would be far more varied than we could have imagined. We could not have envisioned that one day we would have the privilege of ministering in so many parts of the world. But over the years, we have been able to visit different countries in Africa, Asia, and Latin America to see the amazing growth of the church and the indigenous missionary movement in those continents. We have been inspired by the faith and dedication of Christians we have met and we have learned so much from them.

It hasn't always been easy but we have been aware of God's grace, guidance, and provision throughout. In spite of our weaknesses, we have realised that God has graciously been at work. It has been a privilege to be able to work together, sharing our contrasting gifts and encouraging each other in hard times. We have seen the effectiveness of Christians working together in unity, across denominational barriers and in partnerships between mission agencies and national churches.

Although we were initially reluctant to tell our story, we have done so because we wanted to record how the prayers of God's faithful people have been answered, and to share with the next generation our experience of working and witnessing in another culture.

We do not see ourselves as being special or different from other Christians. Jesus calls each of us to know him and to serve him. He gives each of us gifts and opportunities. The command he gave to those first disciples applies to everyone who claims to follow him. We pray that this book may encourage you in your walk with Jesus, and that as you grow in your relationship with him, you will be willing to serve him by playing your part in making disciples – whether it is in your Jerusalem or whether it means going to the uttermost parts of the earth.

We are very grateful to those who have prayed for us and supported us over the past fifty-plus years. We want to thank those who encouraged us to write our story, especially Lee Choy Ping and

Rose Dowsett, and we are indebted to the friends who took so much trouble to read the first draft and made so many helpful suggestions: Petra Abbott, Stan and Gill Bruce, Hugh and Lesley Reynolds, and Peter and Alison Turnpenny. We are also grateful to our three children, Andrew, Ruth, and Catherine, for reading through the initial draft, for sharing their memoires, and making helpful comments. They learned some things they never knew!

Lastly, we owe so much to Reuben Grace, the content and media coordinator in the UK of OMF International, and to Joshua Wells, senior commissioning editor at Lion Hudson, for their advice and editorial skills. We also want to thank Miranda Lever for her help with the final editing, Drew Stanley for thoroughly proofreading, and Louise Titley, senior project editor, for all her guidance and encouragement in enabling us to complete the writing of this book.

There are many others, whom we have enjoyed working with but have not been able to mention by name: colleagues, former students, and friends who have been such an encouragement to us. We appreciate each of you. Above all, we are grateful to God for his grace, his forgiveness, his blessing, and for the privilege of being able to play a small part in the work of his kingdom.

List of Abbreviations

AEAM	Association of Evangelicals of Africa and Madagascar
ANCC	All Nations Christian College
CBCS	Columbia Bible College and Seminary, USA
CIM	China Inland Mission
CIU	Columbia International University
CMJ	Church's Ministry among Jewish People
COMIBAM	Ibero-American Missionary Cooperation
DTC	Discipleship Training Centre, Singapore
GMTC	Global Missionary Training Center, Korea
IEM	Indian Evangelical Mission
IMA	India Missions Association
IMTF	International Missionary Training Fellowship
JFJ	Jews for Jesus
LBC	London Bible College
LCJE	Lausanne Consultation on Jewish Evangelism
OMF	Overseas Missionary Fellowship
OMSC	Overseas Ministries Study Center, USA
OTI	Outreach Training Institute, India
SAMS	South American Missionary Society
SJSM	St John's–St Margaret's
TSM	Theological Seminary of Malaysia
TTC	Trinity Theological College, Singapore
WEAMC	World Evangelical Alliance Mission Commission

Chapter 1
Called to Mission

David and Rosemary, Singapore 1996

*He appointed twelve that they might be with him
and that he might send them out to preach.*

Mark 3:14

*Now this is eternal life: that they know you, the only
true God, and Jesus Christ, whom you have sent.*

John 17:3

Rosemary's story

When David proposed to me one sunny Sunday afternoon in July 1964, he had two conditions. One was that I would cook him green vegetables, since he knew that I didn't like them and never ate them myself. The other was that I would be willing to go anywhere in the world to serve God. This second condition was confirmation to me that this gorgeous guy whose company I so enjoyed was the right person for me to marry.

As we look back, it is both wonderful and surprising to see how God had prepared us with the same sense of calling leading up to that July day. Just as with Jesus' first disciples, the time of knowing him before they told others about him was an important time of preparation. Jesus wanted them to spend time with him, to get to know him, to understand who he was and why he had come. Only after they had spent three years with him, had witnessed his resurrection, and received the Holy Spirit, did he send them out into the world to tell others what they had seen and heard. So, our story begins with an account of how we came to believe in Jesus, how we heard his call to be involved in his mission to the world and how, when we met, we discovered we shared the same faith and the same sense of calling.

From the age of thirteen, I had felt that God wanted me to be a missionary, to tell people about Jesus and to teach the Bible, probably in Africa. I was not very religious as a child although I had gone to Sunday school from the age of four, and to church from the age of seven. When I was five, we went on holiday to North Wales, but I refused to go to church with the rest of the family or to the beach mission for children. I said that I was on holiday! When I was about eight, my friend and I were such a nuisance to our Sunday school teacher that we were separated and put in different groups. When I was eleven, I heard my father and another church leader talking about the myths of the Bible. I knew that "myths" were untrue stories, so I concluded that the Bible was not to be believed, and that I had been deceived about its trustworthiness. At primary school where children were always forming societies,

I started a club to prove that Jesus Christ did not exist. The only person who showed any interest in the club was the other girl who attended Sunday school with me. I am not sure that we ever had an official meeting of the club. At church, I would recite the Apostles' Creed, as I was expected to do, but I would omit the first two words, "I believe".

In 1952, during my first year at grammar school, I heard about meetings of a Junior Christian Union, but stayed well away. Although I was doing well at school, some things were beginning to worry me. I was not sure if my parents really loved me, although with hindsight I realised they loved me very much and tended to spoil me, as I was so much younger than my sister and brother. In my second year, when I was thirteen, I chose to attend some special meetings at church for my age group during the period of Lent. I cannot remember why I decided to do this, but I must have had a growing sense of spiritual interest or need.

We were encouraged to learn verses from the Bible, including Proverbs 3:5–6: "Trust in the Lord with all your heart and lean not on your own understanding...." I received a copy of John's Gospel, which had daily readings, and began to read a short passage most evenings. When I finished, I started again. On reaching John 10 where Jesus says: "I am the good shepherd. The good shepherd lays down his life for the sheep," I kneeled down by my bed and asked Jesus to be my good shepherd, Saviour, and Lord. I felt that I did need someone to look after me and to be my shepherd, but I knew that if I asked Jesus to be my Saviour, he would also have to be my Lord. The teaching I had received from church and from the religious education teacher at school had been very thorough and I understood that you could not just ask Jesus to look after you, but you had to give your whole life to him if you wanted to be his disciple.

In the next few months, I became convinced that God wanted me to be a missionary. My form teacher was surprised when she asked me what I wanted to be when I grew up, and I replied, "A missionary!"

She seemed to think I would get over it. When I looked back in later years, I wondered what or who had given me that idea. Was it because that was what I thought committed Christian women did? Certainly, there was no shortage of missionaries around me.

The lady worker at our church was a retired missionary, and when I was ten and in bed with chickenpox, she had given me a book, called *John and Jeeva of India*[1], which told a story about children in India. I was fascinated by what I read and wanted to learn more about people who lived in other parts of the world. My friend's aunt was a missionary in Burma. We had visiting speakers at church who were missionaries in Africa and South America. In my room I had a picture of Jesus surrounded by children of different nationalities. I always loved the chorus,

> *Jesus died for all the children,*
> *All the children of the world;*
> *Red and yellow, black and white,*
> *All are precious in his sight:*
> *Jesus died for all the children of the world.*

I know such a song may no longer be considered politically correct but it moved me in my childhood to have a concern for the whole world.

Over the years, my desire to be a missionary grew stronger. As a teenager, I read many missionary biographies and imagined myself sitting under a palm tree telling children about Jesus, like Mary Slessor, the Scottish woman who at the age of twenty-eight went to West Africa as a missionary. I was also very moved by the story of Jack Turner, a missionary who worked in the Arctic, but I always hoped Jesus would call me to Africa, not the Arctic.

To prepare for life as a missionary, I wanted to do Religious Education at O-level, but was told it was not an academic subject. I tried to do the subject for my A-level, but was persuaded that it was not considered academic by good universities. My form teacher advised me to study English for my first degree, and, since I was keen to do religious education, to take theology as a second degree when I was older. When my A-level results came out, I was in for a surprise. The results were not good enough for me to be accepted for English.

Why did I do badly at A-level when I had been expected to do well? It had certainly been a very busy year as I was head girl and that brought with it lots of responsibilities. My mother thought that I had spent too much time captaining the hockey and tennis teams, debating at the current affairs society, running the Christian Union, and doing some drama. At the same time, my father was in hospital when I was preparing for my exams, and numerous visitors and telephone calls often interrupted my studying. I began to realise that I was not as clever as my older sister, who got a scholarship to university when she was seventeen, or my brother who had done engineering at Cambridge. As I look back over this time, I realise that if I had passed those exams, I would have gone to university a year earlier than I did, and then I would never have met David. So I am grateful to God for the delay!

I stayed on at school for an extra year and was again appointed as head girl. When I took my A-levels for the second time, I achieved good enough grades to go to Bristol University. There I enrolled for a general Arts degree, which included English and Religious Studies. When there was a clash of subjects in the timetable I made it clear to the head of the theology department that I wanted religious studies to be my priority. He asked why I was not pursuing a degree in theology. I replied, "That is what I have always wanted to do." Within a couple of hours, I found myself starting a BA in Theology, which included a study of the biblical languages. I immediately saw the change of course as God's guidance and the preparation I needed to teach the Bible.

I struggled with some aspects of the theology course at university. Whereas some lecturers, like Alec Motyer, Mike Farrer, and John Wenham, increased my understanding of the faith and gave me a great love for the Scriptures, others left me rather confused. In

17

the first lecture I attended on the Pentateuch, the lecturer kept talking about four characters called "J", "E", "D", and "P", which he described as the four sources behind the first five books of the Bible. I hadn't a clue what he was talking about or who they were.

For over a year, I attended the university church, but was disappointed that those who spoke did not seem very certain about their faith. In my first term I had decided to become involved in the Christian Union where those I met, and those who gave talks – like Peter Dawes and Stafford Wright – seemed to have a clearer understanding of what it meant to be a Christian. My school had advised me to join the Student Christian Movement at the university. I went for a few meetings but was surprised when the small group of students were discussing the Apostles' Creed. They seemed very unsure of what they believed. I started to attend, and subsequently led, Bible studies in my hall of residence. I really enjoyed these and learned many lessons about leading small groups, which would become a major part of my future ministry.

I shared a room with a student from Yugoslavia, who tried to help me understand something of the differences between my culture and her culture. She wanted me to learn words in the Macedonian language, but I was learning Hebrew and Greek at the time and couldn't cope with another language. Since then, I have realised how much it would have meant to her if I had tried. Sharing with her stimulated me to join prayer meetings for international students and for missionary work in Africa.

After completing my degree, I decided to do a postgraduate teaching course to equip me, first to teach religious education at a grammar school up to A-level, and then to work in Africa. I was focused on gaining my teaching qualification when I signed up for the Postgraduate Certificate in Education (PGCE) course at Bristol University, but I got more than I expected.

I met an earnest young man named David on the first day of the course. Unlike me, he had been educated at private schools and seemed rather serious, but I soon discovered that he had a sense of humour and was fun to be around. We were in the same group for everything because we were doing the same special subjects. Like me, David was a committed Christian and interested in the possibility of working overseas. He volunteered to help me with the Christian group I was setting up in the department. I began to see that we had many things in common.

By the end of the course, we had become good friends but nothing more. Finally, on the night I was leaving Bristol for an interview to teach at a grammar school back in the Midlands, he asked if we could write to each other. I was delighted at this glimmer of hope. A few weeks later, he invited me to visit him and his parents near Bath. David had been working as a plasterer's mate in a building company to earn some money. As we drove past the company office, I casually remarked that one day I would be able to say that I used to know someone who worked there. This obviously worried David because I was implying that the day would come when our friendship would end. The following day he took me to Victoria Park in Bath and asked me to marry him. I was speechless, but at least he took my silence as a positive response. He has always claimed that I never actually said "Yes!"

David's story

I grew up in a vicarage in Bristol. As a young boy, I wondered what I might like to do in the future. Like many other seven-year-old boys, I imagined it would be exciting to become a fireman and race around the city sounding the siren, or a policeman telling people what to do, especially those I did not like. These were a young boy's dreams, but they quietly ended one winter evening.

That evening, I was wandering around the garden by myself, and stars began to come out. As the evening grew darker, more and more stars began to fill the sky. I don't know what took hold of me, but I found myself thinking God must be very great if he could create such an amazing universe. I was so overwhelmed by the thought of God's greatness that I kneeled down on the grass and told him I wanted to serve him with my life. It was a simple, childlike prayer, but it changed my life forever. Gone were my ideas of being a fireman or policeman, replaced by ideas of serving God.

The next morning at breakfast, I precociously announced to my family, "I am going to be the Archbishop of Canterbury." I told my parents and two older brothers that I was going to be a vicar and was aiming for the top job. They all laughed and told me I would soon get over it, but I was not put off. I started to build a simple chapel in the garden and invited my brothers to come and hear me preach. They refused, but a number of chickens came out of curiosity, so I had some sort of congregation. The chickens were all converted but, alas, only into dinners, and their numbers diminished as one by one they provided meals for the family. I was learning an important lesson about Christian ministry and church growth and the need to preserve your flock!

My father had come to accept Christ as his saviour as a young man and felt God's call to the ordained ministry. His sincere faith had a deep impact on my life and his example undoubtedly had an influence on my choice to follow him into the ordained ministry. When I was ordained in St Paul's Cathedral in London, it meant a great deal to me that my father was present and took part in the ordination ceremony. A few months before he died, we shared a precious moment together, when he told me that he was looking forward to seeing Jesus after he died.

My mother also had a strong faith when she was young. As a teenager, she attended Holy Communion every day at her church in Luton. She did this for one-and-a-half years. For a long time, she had a desire to be a missionary in India. But after they were married, she did not find it easy to be a vicar's wife and, over time, she became less sure of her faith and more critical of Christians.

As I was growing up, my family gave me the nickname of "Bunk" after a character in a popular series of children's books about a little boy called Bunkle, who was always getting into trouble. Apparently, my parents used to tell my brothers to "Go and find David and tell him not to do it!" I do not think I was a particularly naughty or difficult child but, at the age of seven, I was sent to a boarding school, along with my brother Richard. I continued to study at boarding schools until I was nearly nineteen. I was never told why my parents chose this path of education for my brothers and me. I suspect the reasons were both financial and practical. My mother was convinced we would benefit from being educated at private schools rather than in the state system. With us in boarding schools, she was also able to concentrate on her role as a teacher and at the same time make a substantial contribution to the family finances.

At the age of thirteen, I gained a scholarship to an independent school called St John's, Leatherhead, founded to provide a good education for the sons of clergy. At this point in my life, I was still thinking of being ordained and enjoyed the regular services in the school chapel. I attended a group called the Vivian Redlich Society, named after a former student at St John's who served as a missionary in New Guinea and was among a group of missionaries who were stabbed and beheaded by the Japanese during the invasion of those islands. While a student at St John's I was confirmed as a member of the Anglican Church by my godfather, who was then the bishop of Guildford. I remember expecting at least some kind of tingling sensation when the bishop laid his hand on my head, and was somewhat disappointed when I felt nothing.

When I was eighteen, I had six months to spare before going to university and found a job teaching in a small boarding school outside Bristol. On discovering that two of the teachers at the school met on a regular basis to pray for the boys, I was curious and asked if I could join them. I was not used to unscripted prayer, but I was fascinated by the way they talked to God in an intimate manner and by the concern they had for the schoolboys. They lent me some books by the British evangelist, Roy Hession, who had personal experience of the East African revival in the late 1920s and 1930s. The books were an eye-opener for me, giving me a clearer understanding of what Christ had achieved on the cross and what it meant to be his disciple.

During the summer, I was unexpectedly invited to be a junior officer at a Christian camp organised for young teenagers. The camp was meant to provide the youngsters with an adventure holiday in the beautiful Somerset countryside. It also featured a series of talks explaining what it meant to be a Christian. As I listened to the talks, I realised more clearly than ever before that Christ had died for me and that I did trust him as Lord and Saviour. This did not make my childlike prayer at the age of seven or my Anglican upbringing any less meaningful. If anything, it was an endorsement of my life of faith up till now. It clarified my thinking and gave me a strong desire to find out as much as I could about following Christ when I went to university.

I was accepted to read Classics and Theology at Cambridge in 1960. My three years there flashed by all too quickly but they had a huge impact on my life. I enjoyed the fellowship and preaching at the Round Church. Week by week I heard passages of scripture carefully explained and applied to everyday life. I enjoyed my studies, though I struggled with the teaching of the more liberal lecturers in the theology faculty. I learned much through the scholarship and humility of Professor "Charlie" Moule, who always required his class of 200 students to stand for prayer before he began a lecture. I was very encouraged by the Christian Union and met many students who were deeply committed in their faith. It was such a privilege to listen to some of the ablest Bible expositors in the country, and I inherited from them a deep love of the Scriptures. I read books about missionary heroes like Hudson Taylor, the founder of the China Inland Mission (CIM) in 1865, and the Cambridge Seven who later went out to work with him in China. Little did I know that nearly forty years later I would work with the same mission and become the ninth general director.

At Cambridge, along with other members of the Christian Union, I was challenged to consider the possibility of working overseas as a missionary. I had heard a number of missionaries talk about their work overseas and I had read many missionary biographies. I began to wonder if God was calling me to ministry overseas, and if so, where would I go? I had led a monthly prayer meeting for China, but realised there was no way in the 1960s that someone from Britain could go as a missionary to communist China.

One Saturday night, following a week's programme on world mission held at the Round Church, I became convinced that God was calling me to work abroad. Kneeling down beside my bed, I committed my life to serving God in overseas mission, and asked for his guidance on where I should go. The next morning, I heard a sermon preached by the head of a mission about ministry to the Jewish people. I was so surprised by this immediate answer to my prayer that I rushed up to the preacher after the service and asked him about the prospect of working with his mission. His response was not what I expected. He was extremely discouraging. He told me that Jewish ministry was highly sensitive and very difficult, and that his mission did not have the resources to engage new workers. He said that I lacked the necessary qualifications and experience. I should finish my degree, do ordination training, and get some experience of ministry in the UK first before thinking about serving overseas. It might be useful to get a teaching qualification as well, he added.

I was dismayed by his comments, but not totally discouraged. I determined to gain the necessary qualifications and experience. During the summer vacation, I travelled to Israel because I wanted to visit some of the places where key biblical events had taken place and because Israel had become the national home for Jewish people from around the world. I spent several weeks in a kibbutz[2] near Beersheba and was surprised to learn that most of the kibbutzniks were secular rather than religious Jews. Most of them came from Eastern Europe and had sought sanctuary in Israel from Nazi persecution. Although they had escaped from the Holocaust, many of their relatives had died in German concentration camps. This bitter experience made it difficult for them to believe in a loving God. A teacher from Poland gave classes in Modern Hebrew for anyone who came to live or work in the kibbutz. He inquired about my plans after completing my university course. When I said I was thinking of being ordained, he remarked, "Then you believe in God?" Another time he offered to show me the cows that belonged to the kibbutz which were down in a valley. It turned out the cows were pigs! That was hardly a kosher kibbutz.

I followed the advice I had been given and went to Bristol University to study for the PGCE, as this would be a useful qualification to have for service overseas. I met Rosemary on the first day of term. She was in the same group of six who had chosen Religious Education as their main subject. We attended the same lectures and saw a lot of each other. We chatted often and I enjoyed her company. I learned she was a committed Christian, who had read theology at Bristol University. She lived in a flat near the university, and I found it convenient to join her and her flatmate for a sandwich lunch some days. Over the months, our friendship deepened.

When the last day of the course arrived, I was uncertain as to whether our relationship would continue. A group of students who were Christians opted to go to Cheddar Gorge, a nearby scenic spot, rather than attend the end-of-course party where drinks would be flowing too freely. I drove the group to the top of the gorge and dropped them off. After parking my mother's car at the bottom of the gorge I walked up to join the other students. As they came towards me, Rosemary climbed onto a stile, jumped off and said, "Catch me," which I was very happy to do!

After our walk in the gorge, I drove the others back to their homes. This left Rosemary and me alone in the car. When we arrived at her flat, I got out of the car and we chatted for a while. It was a lovely June evening and although it was quite late, it was still warm and light. I was unsure what to say when I realised that I might not see Rosemary again. There was a long pause in our conversation. Eventually, I asked her if she would be willing to write to me. Then I added, "You never know. In a year's time, we might be in love with someone else!"

A few weeks later, Rosemary came to visit me in my parents' house. I had been earning some money working on a building site and, as we drove past the place where I was working, she remarked, "One day I shall be able to say that I knew someone who used to work there." I did not like the fact that she referred to our relationship in the past tense. I had realised for some time that we shared the same trust in the Lord Jesus and that we both felt called to serve God in mission. The time had come to put our relationship on a permanent footing. So I proposed, and the rest is history!

Chapter 2
Together in Mission

*Our wedding at Clifton Theological College,
23 July 1966*

*Trust in the Lord with all your heart and lean not on
your own understanding; in all your ways submit to
him, and he will make your paths straight.*

Proverbs 3:5–6

Rosemary and I shared the same conviction that God was calling us to work overseas, but we needed to be fully prepared. While we were engaged, Rosemary taught Religious Education at Tipton Grammar School in the heart of the Black Country. It stood between the largest gasworks in Europe, a cemetery, cooling towers, and slag heaps. She doesn't remember seeing much sun, but she chose to go there because she wanted to help children from under-privileged backgrounds to realise their true potential. She also saw this as a time to develop her gifts in teaching before going to teach overseas.

I went to Clifton Theological College to study more, prior to being ordained in the Anglican Church. There were several colleges I could have joined, including Ridley College in Cambridge, where my father had done his ordination training. I chose Clifton because the lecturers were known for their commitment to scripture and careful exposition of the biblical text. I wanted to study the Bible and learn how to make its message relevant to modern life. There were a number of courses on doctrine, church history and liturgy, which we were required to study in preparation for the ordination exam. I particularly appreciated the detailed exposition of individual biblical books, including the study of the Hebrew text of Isaiah and the Greek text of 1 Peter. Because I had studied classics and theology for my first degree, my programme was not as heavy as it was for other students. It was possibly for this reason that in my second year I was appointed head student. It also meant I had more time to do my own private study of the Scriptures. In particular, I studied the lives of the patriarchs in Genesis, and over the years, I have developed this material into recorded sermons for Ethiopian Christians, lectures in Bible colleges, and a book.

There were a number of practical sessions, supposedly preparing us for parochial ministry. I remember one session, led by the principal's wife, on funerals and how to lay out a dead body – a skill I never had to use! I don't recall courses on mission or evangelism, but there were courses on elocution and homiletics. I was looking forward to the latter, as I certainly wanted to learn how to preach. In the event, my early attempts at preaching were not very successful. As part of the homiletics course, every student had to preach a sermon in front of his colleagues. The vice-principal, who taught the course, then commented on the content and style of the sermon. When it came to my turn to preach, he said my sermon was devotionally helpful but theologically a muddle!

Rosemary too did not think very much of the first sermon she heard me preach. I was speaking about the evidence for the resurrection. She said, "It was sweet, but not very clear." There was a bright note though. I went to speak at a Pentecostal church in Wales as part of the weekend ministry, arranged for the students at Clifton as part of their training. After the sermon, a lady said, "Your preaching is just like John Stott's!" I felt a surge of pride and encouragement, until the lady continued, "He hasn't got the power either." I later recounted this experience to John Stott and he was most amused.

One of my fellow students boasted that his wife would be able to type his sermons and I responded jokingly that since my wife had a degree in theology, she would be able to write mine. Another student, John Goldingay, had studied at Keble College, Oxford, where he gained a first in theology. At first sight, he didn't seem a typical candidate for ordination. He had a Beatles haircut, even before the Beatles, and read the *New Musical Express*. What neither of us knew when we started the course at Clifton was that we would serve together as curates in the same parish in North London and I would be best man at his wedding. Later, John became principal of St John's College, Nottingham, then Professor of Old Testament at Fuller Theological Seminary in Pasadena, USA, and author of numerous books. In retirement, he has completed a three-volume work on Old Testament theology.

Married in the college chapel

Rosemary's father died the year before we were married and her mother would have found it upsetting to have the wedding at St Philip's church in Wolverhampton, where Rosemary grew up and where he had been church warden. We decided to get married in Bristol, where we had met and studied together. We were married in the small, rather unpretentious building serving as the college chapel. A few years later it was used as a games room and, subsequently, as a bicycle shed.

We spent our honeymoon in the USA, which gave people the impression we were incredibly rich. Nothing could have been further from the truth. The problem was that I was about to become a curate at Christ Church in North Finchley, London, and we had two months after our wedding before we could move into the curate's house. We did not think that living with in-laws was the best way to start our married life, but we could not afford to live anywhere else. Graham Cliff, a friend from college, invited me to be the best man at his wedding in Pennsylvania. He arranged for us to have accommodation and an allowance for several weeks while taking part in a US government youth programme in Washington DC. The flight across the Atlantic in a turboprop Bristol Britannia seemed to take forever – thirteen hours with a stop in Newfoundland – but it only cost £59 each for a return ticket. We used all of Rosemary's savings from two years' teaching to pay for the tickets. The flight from Heathrow was delayed twenty-four hours, so we had to stay overnight in London. We thought it wouldn't be difficult to find a room in such a big city. We had forgotten that the next day England were playing in the semi-final of football's World Cup at Wembley, so we struggled to find a room, but eventually found a small one, the last available, in a hotel near Euston station.

Living in the servants' quarters

When we returned from America, we moved into our new home in North London. It had originally been the servants' quarters of the large Victorian vicarage which housed the vicar, the Revd Harold Parks, and his family. Mr Parks, as we called him, had preached at the college chapel, and his sermon made an impression on me. He said that when God appeared to Moses in a burning bush, he could have used any bush in which to display his glory. In the same way, he went on to explain that God could use anyone he chose to fulfil his purposes, even though we might feel insignificant and inadequate. Even though with hindsight I am not sure that this is the main point that comes out of Moses' encounter with God, I found what he said a real encouragement to me as I contemplated the beginning of my ministry at Christ Church, North Finchley.

Rosemary and I were also attracted to the parish because there was a significant Jewish population in the area, which tied in with my concern for Jewish people to come to know Jesus as their Messiah. We went for our interview with the vicar armed with a list of questions that I had been advised were relevant to ask when looking for a curacy. Rosemary was surprised to see it included questions about days off and holidays. As it turned out, the vicar anticipated all my questions before we needed to ask them. This encouraged us to believe God was calling us to serve in this church for the next three years.

Mr Parks took a great deal of trouble to train his curates and help them develop their gifts. He gave John Goldingay, the other curate, and myself specific areas of responsibility and then trusted us to carry out our roles. He spent a lot of time helping us learn how to develop our ministry. He did not initially ask us to take weddings or funerals. First, he would let us observe him as he took the ceremony. Then he would allow us to take part of the service, and only then would he give us the responsibility of taking these services on our own. He was like a master craftsman, patiently training his apprentices. We were extremely grateful for the time and energy he invested in our development. It provided a great model for us to follow when we found ourselves in positions of leadership and responsibility.

In a previous church he had experienced a breakdown as a result of overwork and the stress of parochial ministry. He shared quite openly about the length of time it had taken him to recover from his breakdown and he was determined that those he trained would not go through the same traumatic experience. He insisted that his curates took a day off each week, had a week off after Christmas and Easter, and had at least three weeks' holiday in the summer. His philosophy was that if you gave your staff sufficient time to rest, you could expect them to work hard when they were at work.

He was concerned for the health and well-being of those who worked with him.

In other ways, our first three months at Christ Church were not so easy. The house was suffering from rising damp, which needed to be treated. The kitchen still looked as it did when it was built in the nineteenth century. We were not able to unpack all our belongings and for some time the plumbers and decorators were working around us. It was impossible to get the house as straight as we would have liked, but the vicar was sometimes critical of the state of our home. His own wife was an experienced and highly organised mother and housekeeper, who was helpful to Rosemary. His criticism of us left me very discouraged. What helped us cope during this difficult time was the confidence that this was where God wanted us to be.

Early on Mr Parks told me I must wear my dog collar at all times. At the last harvest supper, when we were leaving the church, I showed the parish a (very respectable) picture of me in the bath wearing my clerical collar to show how obedient I'd been! Interestingly, the vicar did not make the same demand on John Goldingay, my fellow curate. I concluded he was slightly afraid of what John might say!

The disastrous sermon!

The vicar laid stress on the importance of teaching God's Word, and I received some invaluable training in preaching. If I was scheduled to preach on a particular Sunday, I would have to give him the complete manuscript of my sermon on the preceding Thursday. On the Saturday, I was required to preach in front of him in an empty church. He would then go over the sermon and make suggestions to improve it. For example, he would suggest I had more illustrations or clearer headings. The process was intimidating, but I appreciated his willingness to invest so much time in helping me to become a more effective communicator.

After almost a year, I was no longer required to submit my manuscript to the vicar before I preached, and that was when disaster struck.

It was Trinity Sunday and I had prepared a sermon for the evening service on the last verse of 2 Corinthians 13, "May the grace of the Lord Jesus Christ, and the love of God, and the fellowship of the Holy Spirit be with you all." I had worked hard on the sermon, and felt confident about having done good work. Then, on Sunday morning, the vicar preached from the same passage, making similar points and following a similar outline to the one I had prepared. It was evident we had used the same commentaries. That afternoon I hurriedly wrote a different sermon on the doctrine of the Trinity, not an easy task!

After my preaching, the vicar accosted me in the vestry. He was furious. "That was a terrible sermon," he said. "It was heretical. You were not teaching the doctrine of the Trinity. You were teaching tri-theism. Don't ever preach like that again! If you do, I will walk out of the church." With hindsight, I think I should have gone to the vicar immediately after he had preached his sermon in the morning and explained my dilemma. He probably would have told me not to worry and to preach my sermon anyway.

Rosemary and I were due to go on holiday the next Tuesday, and the vicar told me to think about what he had said. I was devastated. Rosemary was upset that I had not explained to Mr Parks what had happened. On the Monday, she went to the vicar's house to speak with his wife and, making sure that the study door was open and she was within earshot of the vicar, she explained what had happened the previous day. The vicar never made any comment, but after this, our relationship with him began to improve. The next two years we enjoyed working together, and he was very supportive of us in our ministry abroad.

The challenges in ministry

We inherited a huge youth fellowship, designed for those between the ages of fourteen and eighteen. Over 180 went to the annual Easter house party. It was a vibrant ministry and the previous curate had been gifted in developing and training future leaders. The only problem was that many of the young people were now in their twenties and it was time for them to move on. Some were even older than we were. Twelve of them left to get married that summer. My predecessor continued to run house parties and recruited many who had worked with him in the church to help out. His was a wonderful ministry and a great blessing to many, but inevitably, it reduced the numbers at the church house party. This was disappointing from one perspective, but we still had a large youth fellowship of over sixty, whom we sought to encourage and develop.

Together with many other churches in Finchley, we organised large evangelistic rallies in our spacious church hall and these were attended by several hundred young people. A friend from theological college had written a song where a man recounts the story of his life, how from childhood to the grave he repeatedly ignored the claims of Christ. This song presented such a powerful message for young people that we decided to make a set of slides showing the various stages of his life. I then asked Cliff Richard, who attended the neighbouring Anglican church, to record the song for us. I sang the song on tape and sent it to Cliff. He then made a professional recording in his inimitable style.

In the mid-sixties, North Finchley was a typical London suburb with mainly middle-class families and, in consequence, most of the young people at our church were from middle-class backgrounds and attended grammar or private schools. But one of the former members of the Youth Fellowship, Graham Claydon, who later was ordained and became vicar of St Mary's Islington, reached out to other young people, including boys from a residential home nearby. Others belonged to gangs of mods or rockers, two conflicting British youth subcultures of the 1960s. Media coverage meant that they were often perceived by middle-class people as violent, unruly troublemakers. Some of them started coming to our weekly "games" evenings, until the church secretary complained about them damaging the property when kicking a football in the church hall. Graham spent hours drinking coffee and chatting with these young people. Eventually some of them not only came to our house party but also came to accept Jesus as their Saviour. There seemed to be no doubt about the genuineness of their faith. The big question was whether they would fit into our middle-class Anglican church. On the first Sunday after the house party, two of them came to church dressed, not in their usual leather jackets, but in suits. They did not feel very comfortable in this new environment and soon gave up on coming to church.

This made us realise that reaching young people who belonged to their own subculture was as challenging as reaching those who came from another country or a totally different background. In evangelism, the good news of Jesus needed to be explained to them in terms that were relevant and meaningful. In discipleship, the teaching they were given needed to be geared to the particular challenges and temptations they faced. In worship, they needed to be encouraged to use the kind of music with which they were comfortable. When we were subsequently living in Africa and Asia, we realised the importance of encouraging the use of indigenous musical instruments and patterns of worship. After we returned to the UK, we saw how churches that used contemporary forms of music attracted more young people and enabled them to worship God in a way that was natural to them.

We tried to use our home to welcome any who wanted to pop round or attend a Bible study. This resulted in our settee, our best piece of furniture, being damaged with cigarette burns. We reminded ourselves of the words of George Burton of the Mayflower Family Centre: "people matter more than things!" One Christmas we put up a homeless young person for a few nights, only to discover he was on the run from the police. I later visited him in prison in Wormwood Scrubs!

One year we took a group of twelve potential leaders away for a week together in Wales, and that proved to be a formative time in their lives. Most of them have continued as strong Christians and they have been actively involved in different forms of ministry. Even after fifty years we are still in touch with several of them and appreciate their friendship. Many have commented on how significant that week in Wales was in their own spiritual development.

Spending a week together with a small group allows plenty of time for friendships to develop. As people share in the life of a small community and enjoy common experiences, they become more relaxed and more willing to share at a deeper level. We got to know members of the group better and they got to know more about us. When we went back home and returned to the normal life of the church, there was a stronger bond of fellowship and greater level of understanding. We were learning an invaluable lesson to take with us into future ministry and leadership responsibilities. Just as Jesus spent three years concentrating on twelve disciples, we realised that investing quality time with a small group is an effective way of developing future leaders.

We continued to run the large house party at Easter each year, and it was a great encouragement as we saw young people give their hearts to the Lord. On the first evening of one house party, a girl who was naturally shy accepted Christ and it was wonderful to watch her lose her shyness as she grew in faith. By Tuesday, several other girls had also professed conversion. Three of these had originally planned to come only for the weekend but, after much prayer that they would stay longer, they agreed to come for the whole week. So, it was doubly thrilling when they made their decisions, and it was also great to see them subsequently remaining faithful to those decisions and attending a weekly Bible study.

We made it a priority to encourage the young people in their study of the Scriptures. While at university, Rosemary had spent much time running Bible studies for the Christian Union and the Church of England Society. Now, she invited the teenagers who were keen to explore the Word of God and grow in their faith to come to our home for midweek Bible study. We started with one group; soon there were three. Our home could not accommodate all three groups, so one had to meet in the other curate's home. After a year at Christ Church, our son Andrew was born. Rosemary was thankful that we had already opened our home, which was next to the church, to the young people, and so they continued to spend time in our house and help us by babysitting.

Rosemary had given up teaching in school when we got married because she wanted to be involved in church ministry. She was encouraged by the vicar's wife to start a group for young wives. A group of church members came to our house for Bible study once a fortnight, and the week in between they invited non-Christian friends to come and discuss questions about Jesus. Older ladies ran a crèche for babies and preschool children, and the gatherings on both weeks proved very popular. Rosemary enjoyed being able to run Bible studies and host the ladies' groups in our home while caring for our baby.

Guidance at the eleventh hour

As we began our third year in North London, we were thinking and praying about our future ministry. We both felt called to serve God overseas, but the question was, where? At university I felt God had called me to serve among Jewish people. Rosemary, on the other hand, had felt called from the age of thirteen to teach the Bible to children in Africa. So where were we meant to go? How could these two apparently irreconcilable callings come together? Whose guidance should we follow? Mine, because I was the man? (It was normally assumed at that time that the call and career of the male would take precedence.) Or Rosemary's, because her guidance dated back fourteen years?

As we contemplated how to resolve our dilemma, we saw the unfolding of God's guidance. In September, we were scheduled to attend two different interviews to explore ministry opportunities. In the morning we went to see Bill Curtis, who had talked about ministry among the Jewish people when I was a student in Cambridge. He was no more encouraging now than he had been years before. Even though I was now qualified and had done everything he had suggested to get training and experience, I was told the society, the Church's Ministry among Jewish People (CMJ), had no money to send out new workers. He suggested Rosemary could work as the headmistress of CMJ's school for Jewish girls in Teheran, but he did not know what I could do!

In the afternoon we went for an interview with the South American Missionary Society (SAMS). They were looking for young couples who could serve as Bible teachers in Latin America where the churches were growing very quickly but where many Christians had only a superficial knowledge of the Bible. The Revd Bob Smith with whom we spoke was very positive about our serving with SAMS and encouraged us to fill in application papers by early December.

The outcome of the two interviews seemed reasonably clear to us: the door to work among Jewish people was closed, but a new door was opening which we had not seriously considered before – the possibility of working in South America. Surely the opportunity to teach the Bible should take precedence over any geographical preference. So, it was with glad hearts and relieved minds that we concluded this was God's way forward for our lives. Rosemary enrolled for Spanish evening classes.

We thought we knew where we were meant to go, but God clearly had other ideas. A few weeks after our interview with SAMS, our parish hosted an exhibition called "The Bible Come to Life". The exhibition was organised by CMJ. Since I was known to have expressed interest in Christian witness to the Jewish people, I was asked to preach a sermon on the Church's relationship to the Jewish people. Apparently, I preached with such enthusiasm and passion that one elderly parishioner told me that I was obviously called to work among the Jewish people.

Later the same week, a casual question by the Revd Bill Metcalfe, the exhibition director, set into motion a series of events that would have consequences for our future ministry. Bill knew that we had gone for an interview with CMJ a few weeks before and asked me why I was not pursuing the idea of serving with CMJ. When I told him that the society could not afford to send out new missionaries, he suggested we write a letter to the leader of the CMJ team in Ethiopia, which was working among the Falasha Jews, a small minority group of about 25,000 people, who followed an ancient form of Judaism. They were called Beta Israel (House of Israel) or Falasha (meaning "landless wanderers").

Bill knew the work was developing and was sure the team would welcome a new couple. With that encouragement and a sense that it might be right to push this door one more time, we sent a letter to Ethiopia.

The weeks went by and there was no reply. It was already December and the time for us to send in our application to SAMS was fast approaching. We felt we should take a day out to think through what we should do and to pray for God's guidance and conviction. John Goldingay kindly offered to look after our one-year-old, his godson, while we spent the day in prayer and fasting. By the evening, Rosemary and I agreed that if we had heard nothing back from Ethiopia the next day, we would send in our application to work with SAMS in South America.

Much to our surprise, the next morning a letter arrived from Ian Lewis, the team leader of CMJ's work in Ethiopia, saying he would love us to work in Ethiopia, and assuring us that we would be an asset to the team. The same morning, Bill Curtis, who had repeatedly discouraged us from applying to CMJ, called us. He had also received a letter from Ian Lewis, which prompted a rethink of our application. Though the lack of funds for our support was still a concern, he invited us to meet a selection committee to seek God's will for our future.

We were interviewed by the selection committee on a Tuesday in January. The members of the committee could not have been more encouraging, but there was one difficult moment when Rosemary was asked how she would cope with the very basic standard of living in Ethiopia. We had recently driven to Austria and camped for a few nights on the way. It was not an enjoyable experience and Rosemary had declared she would never go camping again. Before she could reply to the question put by the committee, the chairman intervened, "When I was in their home recently, there was lots of camping gear in the hall. They had just been camping. Of course, they will get on fine living in Ethiopia." We said nothing, and the committee went on to recommend our acceptance by the society.

The CMJ General Committee was due to meet on Friday of the same week to consider the recommendation. Bill Curtis still could not see how the society could afford to accept this recommendation unless there was some indication that financial support would be forthcoming. In the intervening three days, the society received two donations towards our support. One was a gift of £100, the other a promise of an annual donation of £100 for every year in which we worked with CMJ. In those days, £100 represented a fifth of a couple's allowance for a year. With these donations, the general committee felt obliged to accept us as mission candidates. God had made his will clear, but at the eleventh hour. He had answered both of our desires because we were going to Africa and we were going to work among Jewish people.

Chapter 3
On the Roof of Africa

Andrew in the Ethiopian Highlands

*The Lord is my shepherd, I lack nothing. He makes
me lie down in green pastures, he leads me beside
quiet waters, he refreshes my soul. He guides me
along the right paths for his name's sake.*

Psalm 23:1–3

Preparing to go

More training? Rosemary and I had studied theology, trained as teachers, and had several years of experience in teaching and ministry. Why did we need more training? That was my immediate reaction when CMJ suggested further training to prepare for missionary service in Ethiopia. Apparently, the leader of the team in Ethiopia had recommended that we would benefit from some practical and relevant courses at All Nations Christian College (ANCC) before going out. He believed that courses on car maintenance, carpentry, tropical hygiene, emergency dentistry, tropical horticulture, hairdressing and photography, among the many practical courses the college offered, would be invaluable to us living in a remote corner of rural Africa.

Those courses were indeed beneficial. It was helpful to have a basic knowledge of vehicle maintenance, especially since there was only one garage in the province where we went to live that served 2.5 million people. The carpentry course enabled me to build a swing and a slide for the children in our small garden. Our attempts at growing our own vegetables were less successful and, fortunately, we were never required to pull out each other's teeth! We were grateful for the practical skills we acquired at All Nations, but we appreciated even more the teaching that helped us to understand, appreciate, and relate to the cultures of other people. It removed our cultural blinkers and stopped us assuming that everything British was normative. In the modern world, ease of travel and digital technology enables us to encounter and, hopefully, appreciate cultures from around the world, but fifty years ago, most of us in the West were not so enlightened.

Since Rosemary already had a degree in theology and there was no nursery that year due to a lack of staff, she was pleased that she would have time to care for Ruth, our newborn baby, as well as a toddler. A friend from the local church kindly looked after Andrew one day a week so she could take a sleeping baby and attend the lectures on mission from David Morris, the principal, who had worked in Nigeria, Lesley Lyall who served in China, and Dr Bill and Shirley Lees who spent many years in Borneo.

We were encouraged to read books on cultural awareness, warning us of mistakes that can be made and the offence that can be caused if we fail to understand and appreciate cultures different from our own. The staff shared stories of the continuing arrogance and cultural insensitivity of some Western missionaries even in the period after the Second World War when most former colonies were gaining their independence. Perhaps one of the most important lessons we learned at All Nations was that it was easy to look critically at the customs and traditions of others while being blind to the weaknesses and bias of our own culture. I remember one lecturer who told us the story of a little girl who went to France with her parents. As she sat at a restaurant waiting for her meal to be served, she observed the way the cutlery had been set out in front of her. "Mummy," she declared, "they have put the spoon and fork the wrong way round." She simply assumed that the way they did things at home in England was the right way and the way the French did things was wrong. It struck me at the time that subconsciously I too had always assumed the way we did things in the UK was correct.

That time of preparation at All Nations helped us to anticipate challenges we would face as missionaries in Ethiopia. It prepared us for the culture shock that comes from being thrown into a totally different living environment, and for the inevitable suspicion, which white people from a former colonial power working in Africa often encounter. Roland Allen's classic *Missionary Methods: St Paul's or Ours?* [1] warned us of the dangers of imposing our traditional Western patterns of worship and styles of leadership on a different culture.

As part of the course I was expected to study the area where we were intending to serve and to learn as much as I could about its history, religion, and culture. We realised that the culture of rural Africa would be very different from that of Britain, but we also came to see that the culture of Ethiopia was very different from other parts of Africa. Much of the country lies on a high plateau, which has provided the country with a natural means of defence and protected it from invasion and colonisation down the centuries. Ethiopians are handsome, proud, and independent people, who perceive themselves to be very different from other Africans.

The Ethiopian Orthodox Church is one of the oldest churches in Africa, dating back to the fourth century, when King Ezana established Christianity as the religion of the country. He had been converted through the witness of a man called Frumentius, a Syrian Greek, who had been shipwrecked with his brother on the coast of the Red Sea. The Ethiopian Orthodox Church places strong emphasis on Old Testament teaching and its followers adhere to practices found in Orthodox or Conservative Judaism. Like some other Eastern Christians, they follow the dietary rules of the Bible, specifically with regard to the slaughter of animals and the prohibition of eating pork. The Church has very distinctive and ancient forms of architecture, music, and liturgy. With a membership of about 36 million people, the majority of whom lived in Ethiopia, it was a founding member of the World Council of Churches. This church dominated the area where our mission was working and, according to the agreement with the Emperor, any Falasha who wished to accept the Christian faith was expected to be baptised into the Ethiopian Orthodox Church.

Some of the most useful advice we received at college came from the principal, David Morris. In one memorable lecture, he warned us of three challenges we would face in missionary life. The first was the challenge of maintaining a vital spiritual life without the fellowship and encouragement of our home church. He encouraged us to make sure we never neglected our personal times of prayer and the study of the Scriptures. He also suggested we ask friends to send us books and tape recordings of Bible teaching. In the twenty-first century, missionaries can access the preaching of some of the most gifted Bible expositors from around the world through the Web at the click of a button. We had no such luxury back in 1970 and were very grateful for the occasional tape or book that arrived through the rather erratic postal service.

The second challenge David Morris cited was the area of sexual temptation. Since Rosemary and I were happily married, we assumed this would not be a problem for us. But Morris wisely said, "Don't you married couples think this will not apply to you!" It was good to be warned. Later, a colleague in Ethiopia said she wished she had had such a warning at her college.

The third challenge was maintaining good relationships. We thought we usually got on well with other people and did not expect personal relationships to be a major problem for us. We could not have been more mistaken.

After completing the course at All Nations, we attended a six-week linguistics programme run by the Summer Institute of Linguistics and held in dilapidated former army barracks in Surrey. While we were there, our toddler, Andrew, and our baby daughter, Ruth, both had measles. That did not help our study and concentration. We both did well at understanding the theory of language learning, phonemics, and principles of grammar, but Rosemary struggled with phonetics. Lecturers sought to encourage her by saying, "You learned your own language." Rosemary replied, "Yes, but it took me five years, and I still have problems pronouncing the letter 'r' and learning to speak other languages."

We expected our visas for Ethiopia to arrive in August. Speakers at college had warned us that if you did not start learning a new language before the age of thirty, you would probably never learn it well. Rosemary was twenty-nine and rapidly approaching her thirtieth birthday. Much to her disappointment the visas did not arrive until October, so we did not leave for Ethiopia until four days after her thirtieth birthday. She jokes that she was a failure before she began.

Arriving in Ethiopia

Before we left the UK in the summer of 1970, some friends and relatives voiced their concerns: "You shouldn't take your children to such a remote part of Africa." It seemed to these well-meaning people that we were selfish and irresponsible to take two small children away from the safety of London and the Home Counties to such a hot climate and deprived area. As we soon discovered, Ethiopia enjoys sunny weather all year round. It claims to be a land of thirteen months' sunshine. For the first three years, we lived in Begemder, a province in the north-west of the country, high up on the Ethiopian plateau, which lies close to the equator. There the weather was warm and sunny for most of the year. However, because of the height above sea level, it was not excessively hot or humid. Our small children could spend much of their time playing out of doors.

Ethiopia is a land of rugged mountains, lakes and rivers and broad savannah. The central plateau ranges in height from 2,000 to 4,000 metres. The edges of this plateau fall away suddenly and dramatically to the lowlands below. The Rift Valley, which runs down the spine of the country, is a remarkable region of volcanic lakes, great escarpments, and stunning vistas. Throughout the country, there is a huge variety of animals with over 800 species of birds, including the beautiful carmine bee-eaters and the bright blue Abyssinian roller. The scenery is covered with numerous indigenous plants and shrubs such as pyracantha, jasmine, and poinsettia. In September, coinciding with the Ethiopian New Year, the landscape is carpeted with the bright yellow national flower, the Adey Abeba, which is seen as a symbol of peace, harmony, and love. For two years, we lived near the Simien Mountains, where in one dramatic location there is a vertical drop of 1,500 metres from the plateau. When we drove from our home to Gondar, the provincial capital of Begemder, we could look down at mountain peaks far below us.

Begemder had a population of about two million, almost all of whom were Amhara, the dominant ruling group in the country at that time, and belonged to the Ethiopian Orthodox Church. Scattered among these was this small group of Falasha, for whom our mission was providing medical services and running a number of schools. Scholars cannot agree about the origin of the Falasha. Some suggest they were an Agau people, converted to Judaism by Jewish traders who travelled across the Red Sea from Yemen. Ethiopian tradition claims the Falasha first came to Ethiopia during the reign of King Solomon. According to the biblical narrative of 1 Kings 10, the queen of Sheba, who had heard of his great wisdom, visited Solomon taking lavish gifts. Ethiopian legend believes she was the queen of Ethiopia and was not only impressed with the king but also had a child by him. When the child, named Menelik, returned to live with his mother, Solomon is reputed to have sent a group of Jews from the tribe of Dan to look after him. The Falasha claim descent from this group of Jewish courtiers.

Understanding the culture

The Falasha observed only the religious festivals described in the Old Testament. They had priests rather than rabbis and retained the practice of animal sacrifice. They lived in small village communities or family groupings scattered over the high plateau of northern Ethiopia. They were friendly and hospitable. On one occasion, when we visited a widow, she insisted on killing her only chicken so that she could give us one of their traditional dishes, even though she had not had the luxury of eating meat for many weeks. When we attended a wedding, we were treated as honoured guests, which we found embarrassing. The wedding feast included a variety of traditional Ethiopian dishes, among which was a kind of beef stew. The local cattle tended to be quite lean with very little fat on them. In consequence, fat was considered a delicacy. Our generous host gathered together all the fat he could find in the stew and to show how he appreciated our presence at the wedding, he offered us the most special dish, which consisted of a plate of cold fat. We tried to show our appreciation for the great honour that was being shown towards us but, not being keen on eating much fat at all, let alone cold fat, we insisted there must be others at the wedding more deserving of such honour!

Like other Ethiopians, the Falasha exhibited a strong sense of community. Whenever there was a wedding or a funeral, everybody would come and rejoice or mourn with the family. Family members, friends, and visitors were greeted with a series of kisses on both cheeks, irrespective of age or gender: three kisses normally, but five or more if you had not met for a long time. Initially this was rather a shock, but it felt quite natural after a while and made us feel we were accepted in the local community.

Our first home in Ethiopia was in a small community, two miles from a gravel road and twenty-five miles from the nearest town. The main part of our house was built of stone by Swiss missionaries, but had been colonised by bedbugs. The dining room and kitchen were made with wood, mud, and straw. Some water was available through an ancient communal pump, the rest from a stream half a mile away. The toilet was a hole in the ground, which occasionally was inhabited by snakes.

We were told that we would need a worker to help with the housework full-time, but the very idea appalled us. A couple who had spent many years in the country explained that even poor families had a servant of some kind, often an orphaned relative. It was pointed out that we would appear to be very mean if we did not employ a worker from the local community. This was a surprising lesson for us. We thought we would appear as rich and superior foreigners if we employed a house-help, whereas the local people would have seen us as refusing to accept a common practice and being unwilling to help poorer people in the community. Rosemary realised later she couldn't have coped with lighting charcoal fires to cook or boil water, cleaning mud floors, or other time-consuming tasks, as well as looking after the children. So, we did employ a lady who lived close by and proved to be very helpful in the house, even though she was not as good a cook as we would have liked!

Another thing we had to get used to was the local diet. The staple food in Ethiopia is made from a fine grain called teff. It is ground into flour and used to make the traditional bread, *injera*, which is like a very large flat pancake, made of fermented bread that complements their exotic spices. It is high in iron content and can taste quite bitter, especially to our unaccustomed Western palates. The ground red pepper, added to meat or vegetables, can be very hot and bring tears to the eyes. For the first three months, we struggled to get used to this new diet and only ate it at lunchtime, eating more traditional English food at other times. We did not have access to the wide range of foods available in the UK but indulged in cornflakes and sausages as expensive and occasional luxuries. Over time our taste buds got used to the local food and we began to enjoy it more and more, especially *doro wat*, a chicken stew served with hard-boiled eggs. Since we left Ethiopia, going out for a meal in an Ethiopian restaurant has been a favourite treat for all the family.

Learning the language

We knew it was important to learn the local language. We could hardly expect to understand people or speak of spiritual things effectively unless we learned their mother tongue. In the year before we left England, we attended a course at the School of Oriental and African Studies in the national language, Amharic, designed for people being sent to work in the capital city, Addis Ababa. We found that the vocabulary was highly inappropriate for us as we were going to a remote rural area, where there was no railway station, university, or embassy, all of which featured prominently in these lessons.

Amharic is a Semitic language, related to Hebrew and Arabic. Some words are identical in all three languages, but Amharic is written from left to right, rather than from right to left as in Hebrew. Amharic is rated as one of the most difficult languages in the world to learn. It has its own script of thirty-three basic characters, which can be combined with seven vowels to form 241 different syllables.

Reading and writing Amharic is difficult but trying to speak it brings its own challenges. It contains a number of plosives, that is, consonants produced by stopping the airflow using the lips, teeth, or palate, followed by a sudden release of air. It was essential that we learned the difference between a consonant that was a plosive and one that was not, although they sounded very similar. The two may sound identical to an untrained ear but are in fact totally different letters.

Learning a new language at any time is a challenge, especially if you are already thirty. When we arrived in our first home, I was given the help of a language teacher, who was the headmaster of the small school in the compound. Meheretie was a keen Christian and we soon became great friends. We met for an hour each morning when he tried to help me understand the language and pronounce the words correctly.

After our hour-long lesson in Amharic, I would spend the rest of the day trying to learn vocabulary and go over what he had taught me. Rosemary, meanwhile, was told to pick up "kitchen" Amharic as best she could while looking after the children. That was a big disappointment for her. It made it difficult for her to study the language seriously. She felt called to be involved in teaching the Bible and had prepared for many years to do so. How could she ever teach the Bible if no provision was made for her to learn the language that people around her were speaking?

We did the best we could and, in time, I found that I was able to teach and preach in Amharic. This did not prevent us making mistakes and causing people to laugh. I once referred to Rosemary as my white ant, instead of my wife! On another occasion, instead of announcing a course that would last for three months, I announced that breakfast would last for three months! My language teacher, Meheretie, would often be reduced to laughter by my pronunciation. On one occasion, when we were on an evangelistic trek, he almost fell off his horse with laughter when I invented a new word that combined the Amharic words for mouth and nose.

The mission

The majority of the Falasha were poor, living in small, scattered communities spread over a wide area in the beautiful but rugged mountain terrain of northern Ethiopia. They survived by subsistence farming on rented land, while a few earned a living through weaving or making traditional pottery. The mission personnel did all they could to serve these scattered communities, providing basic medical services, a mother and baby unit and an eye clinic. They also ran three primary schools and a teacher training school. For many years, the mission had run a Bible school. Families were invited to come and live in what was previously an Italian farm compound and attend a Bible school there. While they learned about the Christian faith, their children would go to the local school. After two years some who attended the Bible school decided to follow Jesus and asked to be baptised. They then stayed for a third year to continue their study before returning to their remote villages, where they were encouraged to start a local fellowship of believers.

The Bible school began because foreigners were not allowed to go out into the countryside to evangelise and so the only way to reach people was to invite those who wanted to do so to come and study the Bible. By the time we arrived there was no such restriction and there were small fellowships of believers in several villages.

It was realised there was a danger of Falasha coming to the Bible school for the prospect of free education and future employment. So, the team decided the Bible school should be closed, now that it was possible to do evangelistic treks, pastoral visits, and short teaching courses.

During our first year, as I became more fluent in Amharic, I went on treks with Ethiopian evangelists across the remote and mountainous countryside. We would visit isolated Christian families to encourage them in their faith and to give evangelistic talks to their neighbours using colourful posters. I found it hard to assess the value of these treks. I am sure the families were glad to welcome us and encouraged that we had come to visit, but it was difficult for me to judge the level of response to the teaching. I hope that our willingness to tramp for many hours under the hot Ethiopia sun to provide fellowship to isolated believers was an encouragement to them.

Once when a member of our mission gave a gospel talk in one of these villages, he asked if anyone had a question. Rather than raising a question relating to what had been said, one man wanted to know why the missionary's wife had hair like a horse's tail. Even after Rosemary and I had acquired a reasonable knowledge of Amharic, we were still acutely aware that it was not easy for us to relate effectively to the subsistence farmers, whose culture and way of life had changed little over millennia.

On one occasion a group of us spent five days visiting former Bible school students. All had been deprived of fellowship and teaching for a long time. One man with whom we stayed said that for five or six years he had been walking in the dark as a Christian, struggling to keep going. "Now," he said at the end of our visit, "because you have come so far and spent a time of fellowship with me, I have light and joy."

With the help of one of the local evangelists, I developed some simple Bible teaching on the life of Abraham in Amharic. I bought some battery-operated cassette recorders to give to Christians living in remote locations with little or no fellowship. Whenever they came into the small town of Dabat, where we lived for our second and third years in the country, we would lend them cassettes containing Bible teaching. We still felt we were only having a limited impact on the remote communities, though we were able to teach the Bible to some of the older children and teachers at the mission schools.

Learning from the culture

Our first two years in Ethiopia left a deep impression on us. First, we learned the importance of relationships. Whereas in the West we tend to be always rushing around to get to the next meeting and having little time to stop and chat, we found that Ethiopians always had time to stop, catch up on news, and ask about the family. People were important and, even if it meant being late for an appointment, they would take time to talk with friends or relatives they met along the way. I was surprised by one man who was invited to attend an interview to become headmaster of a large secondary school. When he arrived very late for his interview he did not apologise but simply explained he had met his aunt on the way to the school. He had not seen her for some time and it was important to find out how she and the members of her family were getting on. I suspect that back in the UK he would not have been given the job, but the interviewing panel, which included the local archbishop, understood and appointed him as headmaster.

Secondly, we soon realised the importance of belonging to a community. People did not just get their identity from their work or their family but from the community to which they belonged. If there was a wedding in the village, everyone would come, even people who lived quite far away. If someone died, everybody who lived in the vicinity would attend the funeral and share in the loud wailing. If they were absent for some reason or other, or if they had moved to live in another part of the country, they would make a point, when they returned or visited the area, of going straight to the bereaved family. Even if their visit was several months after the funeral, they would express their sympathy with tears and loud cries.

Sadly, in Britain, most of us have lost that sense of commitment to the local community and live individualistic lives, often with only tenuous links to our wider families.

Another quality we observed among Ethiopians was their gift of hospitality. Wherever we went in the countryside, even though we were complete strangers, we were welcomed into people's homes. Local beer was often served, which was one of the safest things to drink. Coffee beans were roasted and then thick, sweet coffee was offered in tiny cups. If a meal was served, our host would insist that we ate first before the rest of the family. These people had relatively little in worldly terms, but they were willing to share what they had with whoever came to visit them.

On a personal level, we were learning lessons about evangelism in Ethiopia and the future shape of our own ministry. We began to realise that we were not going to be able to develop the kind of Bible school we had hoped for but, as will become clear in the next chapter, God did eventually provide us with new and unexpected opportunities to give Bible teaching to some who were eager to learn. In terms of local evangelism, we realised that the effectiveness of our preaching and discipling of believers depended in large measure on our understanding of the local culture and our ability with the language. Although I was glad to visit these tiny communities, scattered over the mountains, I knew I would never be able to communicate the gospel as well as the local Christians. It seemed logical for us to concentrate on encouraging and teaching Ethiopian believers who could then teach others. God was slowly helping us to understand where we could be more effective in contributing to the spread of the gospel in the country.

Chapter 4
Tales of the Unexpected

Andrew, Ruth and Catherine with Tsehay,
who attended Bible studies and
whose husband became a believer

*"For my thoughts are not your thoughts, neither are
your ways my ways," declares the Lord. "As the heavens
are higher than the earth, so are my ways higher than
your ways and my thoughts than your thoughts."*

Isaiah 55:8–9

In Isaiah 55, God says, "My thoughts are not your thoughts, neither are your ways my ways." This was a lesson we learned many times over in Ethiopia. We were constantly surprised by the way in which God worked in our lives. We had gone to Ethiopia with expectations of what we would like to do. We had expected to teach the Bible in a Bible school to encourage and train local believers. The one thing we were certain we did not want to do was to teach English or other secular subjects. Although we recognised the value of other academic disciplines, we did not feel that was the ministry to which we were called. In our five years there, we discovered that God had other ideas. We ended up teaching English, Ethiopian history, and modern maths! But years later, we saw that God's ways had been higher than our ways.

Bringing up children

One challenge that faces those who feel called to go and serve in a remote part of the world is whether their children will be OK. Before we left for Ethiopia, some of our friends and relatives questioned whether it was right to take such a young family overseas, because they might contract some dreadful tropical disease and lack the level of medical care they could receive at home. Sometimes we did face serious problems and we were concerned about our children's health, but the experience gave us sympathy with those whom we subsequently trained and welcomed as new members of the mission.

We wondered how Andrew, aged three, and Ruth, a one-year-old, would cope with the new environment. They were bitten by bedbugs and fleas, and often saw and heard small rats scrambling across the roof beams of their bedroom. In the first few months, Rosemary discouraged them from going to watch the goat, which we would be eating, being killed. However, unlike Rosemary who shied away from the experience, the children enjoyed it – this was more than could be said for the goat!

In our first year Ruth suffered many bouts of diarrhoea and sickness. The "Dr Spock" guide to parenting we used in those days advised, "If your child has diarrhoea for more than 24 hours, take them to a doctor." That was not much help to us. The nearest doctor was an hour's drive away in Gondar and the only car available was often being used elsewhere. We prayed much and eventually Ruth regained her appetite and kept her food to herself.

Ruth loved playing with her Ethiopian friends and sharing her toys with them. Occasionally, she would get upset with one of the children. She would walk a hundred metres back to our house, start crying and complain, "Habte Yesus hit me!" After lodging her complaint, she would happily walk back to play with him and the other children again.

On one occasion, she was bitten or scratched by a dog on her forehead, but no adult had seen what had happened. Some people said that the dog was rabid, but the problem was that in Amharic the same word is used to mean "rabid" or "sick". When we sought medical advice at the small hospital in Gondar, we were told: "If the dog is rabid, Ruth should immediately have a course of twelve extremely painful injections in her stomach." The American doctor at the hospital was reluctant to inflict this on a child of almost two, unless it was absolutely certain the dog had rabies. There had been no recent outbreak of the disease in the area, so it seemed unlikely Ruth had been bitten by a rabid dog. But should we take the risk of not using the medicine flown from Asmara to Gondar?

The dog was caught and killed. The hospital said they would send the dog's head to Addis Ababa to test for rabies, but the results would not be known until two weeks later. If the tests were positive, it would be far too late to begin a course of injections to prevent Ruth from dying of rabies. It was a terrible dilemma. The local people did not think the dog was rabid. We listened to advice, prayed, and decided not to proceed with the injections. Thankfully, Ruth did not contract rabies and all was well, but it was an extremely stressful time we would not easily forget.

Catherine, our third child, was born in Ethiopia in a mud hut serving as a guest house, but it was the easiest birth of the three. She was delivered by a very able Irish midwife who was working with the United Nations that year as a trainer of Ethiopian midwives in the Gondar hospital. Our Ethiopian friends loved this new white baby in their midst, though they could not understand why the baby had blond hair, since both her parents had dark brown hair. In Ethiopian culture, small children are allowed to do what they want and Catherine soon learned that she could get away with anything, if we were not around. Once, she decided to paint her face black with charcoal. The lady who helped Rosemary with the housework and cooking told us when she tried to stop Catherine, our daughter refused to listen to her and simply said, "Imbi," which means, "No, I won't stop."

In many ways, we led an idyllic family life. There was no television, computer, or mobile phone. There were none of the distractions and temptations that would face a later generation. Our children spent most of the time out in the sunshine, being resourceful and creative in devising their own games. They liked going to the local town or market, but found that some local people stared at this strange sight of white children and tried to pinch their skin to see what it felt like. For a short while, they had a small deer as a pet and they would laugh as it kept doing the splits when its small pointed hooves slipped on the tiled floor of our second home in Dabat. When we went away one time, we returned to be told it had died. We were sure it had provided a local family with a tasty meal.

Going out in the mission Land Rover or the small Volkswagen always brought great excitement and the children thrived on long journeys on the dusty gravel roads in northern Ethiopia. Once, when driving from Gondar to Addis Ababa, a journey of over 400 miles, Andrew, who was only three, stood in the middle of the back seats singing, "We are going in the car, the car. We are going in the car," for hours on end.

When Rosemary was driving for the first time in Ethiopia, she got the wheels of the car stuck in piles of gravel and managed to tip the VW on its side. Suddenly, we were surrounded by a crowd of Ethiopians, who seemed to appear from nowhere. They did not seem to be surprised to see a car on its side and simply pushed it back onto its four wheels so that we could continue our journey. We were all relieved that we had not been hurt and the car had not been damaged, but the children pleaded: "Daddy, don't let Mummy drive!"

On another occasion, while we were shopping in Gondar, we were caught in a violent dust storm, where we saw a large whirlwind suddenly rushing towards us. Andrew and Ruth were on the back seat of the Land Rover, when part of the roof of an adjacent building came crashing down on the vehicle, shattering its rear window. They saw what was happening, were terrified, and got cut by small pieces of broken glass. Fortunately, none of their cuts were very deep, but for years afterwards, Andrew became very anxious, even hysterical, when he heard the noise of a strong wind. We have recently discovered that Ruth, who didn't show any effect at the time, still remembers it and is afraid of thunderstorms.

Home-schooling

Young missionary families are obviously concerned with their children's education. Will there be a local school they can attend? Should we provide them with home-schooling? Will there be adequate teaching materials? Will it be necessary, at some point, to send them to a boarding school?

We had planned to home-school Andrew when he was five, but at the age of three, finding it difficult to communicate with the local children, he soon became bored and began to read the Ladybird books we had brought from the UK. We had been advised to read only a page or two with him at a time. Andrew, however, took the books away and read them on his own, just coming to us when there was a word he did not understand. The small mission school library, a hundred yards from our home, had some Dr Seuss children's books, like *The Cat in the Hat*, which he enjoyed very much. And so did we!

At the end of our second year, we were unexpectedly asked if we would like to have a short period of leave back in the UK.

The policy of the mission was for us to spend three years in Ethiopia before taking some leave, but it seemed that it would fit in better with the plans of the other members of the team if we took that furlough earlier. Being back in England enabled us to meet many of our prayer partners and speak at some of our supporting churches. Over the next few years, we continued this pattern of short terms of service followed by a few months' home assignment. It was good to meet at least every two years with the churches that supported us and the friends who were praying for us. It also meant that we were only absent from the work in Ethiopia for shorter periods of time and less likely to regress in our language skills.

On our return journey to Ethiopia, we arrived at Heathrow with our many cases, two children, and a baby who had no luggage allowance. The British Airways check-in assistant insisted on weighing our entire luggage, all the magazines we had been given to read, and one of the first lightweight Maclaren pushchairs, which we had in place of a carrycot. In exasperation, Rosemary asked if they wanted to weigh four-month-old Catherine as well! We were confronted with a large additional bill and were so grateful that the home director of CMJ, who had come to see us off, was able to pay the bill.

We packed many school books meant for Andrew's home-schooling for the next two years. Alas, the suitcase containing the books was lost in transit. On learning about this, an English supporter sent Andrew some primary school books. His godfather sent him a set of children's encyclopaedias. Andrew read through the ones that interested him as though they were storybooks. When we asked him about his reading, he could always repeat clearly what he had read. He also discovered and began to devour the Living Bible and the Oxford Atlas. When a friend asked him, "What's the capital of Outer Mongolia?" this precocious five-year-old replied, "The correct name for the country is the Mongolian People's Republic and its capital is Ulaanbaatar!" Rosemary and I had worried about how we would school him but God knew we didn't need to worry.

After three years near Gondar in Begemder province, we were unexpectedly moved to Mek'ele, the provincial capital of the neighbouring province, Tigray, 330 miles from Gondar. This was our third home in three years. We had expected to remain in one place and to settle down in one community, but looking back we see that it opened up new possibilities for the children's education and avoided the need to send them away from home. There was a missionary couple from Ireland and an Indian couple who also had young children. This meant that the three mothers could share the task of providing schooling. The following year, a team of water engineers and their families came from England to try to help solve the famine problem in Ethiopia. One of the wives was paid by the British government to teach their children and she willingly took in our two because their ages were similar. This again delayed the need for our eldest, Andrew, to go to a boarding school in Asmara, Eritrea, a further 200 miles to the north. It had been a painful option to consider for so young a child but, in the end, it was never necessary, because that year, in January 1974, war broke out between Ethiopia and Eritrea, and the school and the border were closed.

Unexpected opportunities for ministry

Our primary motivation for going to Ethiopia was to share the good news of Jesus, but we had discovered that opportunities to do so were relatively few. We ran Bible studies for some of the children who attended our school, but we longed to provide more sustained teaching. In our second year, during a school holiday, Meheretie, my language teacher and the headmaster of the mission school at Jenda, and I planned a short residential Bible teaching course for some young teachers and high school students. What we were about to discover, not for the first time in our lives, was that God may take our plans in a new direction and do something that was totally unexpected.

Children in Ethiopia usually started school later than their counterparts in the UK, and most of them were already well into their late teens. Some had expressed faith in Jesus and others were interested enough in the course to want to attend. Everyone arrived for the course a day early. That in itself was surprising. With the relaxed lifestyle in rural Africa, people tend to come late rather than early. Then, totally unexpectedly, two Ethiopian evangelists turned up at the remote farmhouse where we were holding the course. They were from Addis Ababa, 500 miles away, and were travelling around the country seeking opportunities to teach and share the gospel. They had no idea we were conducting our residential course and we had no idea they were coming. Once they had arrived, however, it seemed right to give them an opportunity to speak to the students. They related so well to the young audience and gave such helpful biblical teaching that we decided to discard the talks we had prepared and let them do the teaching. They spoke in a powerful way and encouraged the students in their faith.

About the same time, Rosemary and I received a visit from Fisseha, a trainee health worker, who asked if he and a group of fellow students living and working in a nearby government clinic could study the Bible weekly in our home. They had come to faith through the Pentecostal student movement in Addis Ababa, which had formed fellowship groups in many towns and cities. That year the government forbade Christians from holding meetings for Bible study and prayer in cities like Gondar, where most of the population belonged to the Ethiopian Orthodox Church. Religious freedom was extended only to the Orthodox, Catholic, and Lutheran Churches. The ban, however, did not apply to us. We had government permission to do Bible teaching and hold services, because Emperor Haile Selassie wanted more Falasha Jews to become Christians and adopt the Orthodox faith.

None of the student nurses or health workers were Jewish, but we were now fifty miles north of Gondar and there was no one to stop them meeting in our home on Sundays. They later asked to meet with us midweek at the clinic for "coffee" – but, of course, with Bible study, they were eager to study God's Word and were prepared to suffer for their faith. The studies increased their understanding of the Scriptures and they were emboldened to reach out to others.

One of the schoolgirls, Tsehay, who came to the services at the mission centre was married to a man who was a local school superintendent. Tsehay's parents had forced her to marry when she was thirteen. She was now only seventeen and had just had her first baby. Her husband had a reputation for drinking, lying, and sleeping around. One Saturday, Rosemary visited Tsehay's home and her husband came into the living room and asked questions about our family and our work. He was so pleasant and polite and seemed so interested that Rosemary invited him to visit us the next day to observe the service and Bible study his wife was attending. He told us later he was not at all interested, but when Rosemary invited him to a meal, he felt he had to attend. But he came not only that week, but the next as well.

Then he asked if he could join the group meeting for "coffee" at the clinic. We had a time for questions during the meeting and I fully expected he would raise something controversial like creation and evolution. Instead, he asked, "I have done so many bad things in my life, can God possibly forgive me?" We sought to assure him that God would forgive him and give him the grace to live a life that would please him. He was so thrilled that he invited the health workers and us to his home in Dabat for another meeting each week. When some locals found out about the meetings, they threw stones at the house, but this man and these young people were undeterred.

Looking back, we saw those Bible studies with the trainee health workers were one of the most fruitful times of ministry during our years in Ethiopia. We had not planned this at all and the mission had not developed any strategy for student work, but God gave us the opportunity to study the Scriptures with these students as well as someone who had considerable influence in the area. We were slowly learning that God's plans were different from ours.

Camping with a princess

When you are living in a very remote place, you do not expect to be playing host to royalty, but within a few years, Queen Elizabeth, the Duke of Edinburgh, and Princess Anne all visited Begemder. When the Duke arrived at Gondar airport, his first comment to the team leader of our mission was, "What are you doing in this godforsaken place?" He then paused and added, "Perhaps that is why you are here!"

When Princess Anne visited, she wanted to see the Simien Mountains. The Simien National Park was renowned for some of its rare wildlife and, as president of the World Wildlife Fund, the princess was eager to see this area for herself. Her lady-in-waiting had already visited this remote region and Her Royal Highness was not going to be outdone by her lady-in-waiting.

On learning that the princess would be making her way up the Simien Mountains, our team leader sent a message to the British embassy asking if the princess would like to be accompanied by a doctor or an interpreter. He was told that she did not require a doctor but would appreciate having someone who could speak Amharic. As Rosemary and I lived only a few miles from the starting point for a trip up the mountains, I was asked if I would be her interpreter. That was how I found myself spending three days trekking up the Simien Mountains with a small party consisting of the princess, her lady-in-waiting, her press officer, her bodyguard, and a national park warden.

The royal party arrived with Princess Anne at the foot of the mountain accompanied by an Ethiopian princess. A barbecue had been arranged, and we found ourselves sitting near Princess Anne. When I left one chair vacant between the princess and myself, she remarked, "Come and sit next to me. I haven't got measles!" There followed a very relaxed and pleasant conversation. That day happened to be 14 February, the day celebrated in some countries as Valentine's Day, when admirers often send cards, sometimes anonymously, to someone they love. As a home-school exercise, Rosemary got Andrew, our five-year-old son, to create a simple Valentine's card for the princess. When we gave it to her, she smiled and exclaimed, "Oh, it's not that day, is it?"

Early the next morning, our small party set out, accompanied by a group of local farmers carrying very ancient rifles. In theory, they were meant to provide some sort of protection but since the safety catch on the rifles always seemed to be off, they looked more like a threat than a provision of security. This trek up the Simien Mountains was nothing like the treks I had done before. Each day, as we travelled up the mountain range, tents and tables were carried on ahead, while food and refreshments were flown by helicopter from the hotel in Gondar. One of the porters had the responsibility of carrying the royal commode, which resembled a large piano stool. Every day he would walk past the royal party, proudly bearing it on his head.

Each night, we were housed in deluxe tents, with camp beds, Dunlopillo mattresses, and gas fires. I shared a tent with Princess Anne's bodyguard. On the first night we both emptied the contents of our pockets onto the small table between our beds. The bodyguard put his revolver on the table, and I placed my New Testament next to it.

The scenery in these mountains, where the highest peak rises to over 15,000 feet, is breathtaking. It was a pleasure to be trekking through such dramatic countryside, to catch sight of colobus monkeys, the Simien fox, and the endangered walia ibex, and to enjoy barbecues on the roof of Africa. It was also a privilege to spend those few days in the company of a princess, who expressed her thanks that I had taken time off my "good work" to accompany her. As a missionary, you never know what experiences lie in wait for you!

Sharing the gospel and caring for those in need

One of the tensions that confronts those engaged in mission is how to maintain a balance between evangelism and social action. In scripture we are commanded both to make disciples and to care for the physical needs of others. We can be so concerned to evangelise that we ignore the desperate needs of those around us. On the other hand, we can be so overwhelmed with caring for the sick or the homeless that we never have time to talk about Jesus.

There was some disagreement within the mission as to how much time, energy, and finance should be devoted to medical work and how much to evangelism, discipleship, and Bible teaching. We were a small team of only eight people, which included a medical doctor and two nurses. They were doing a marvellous job providing medical services, pre- and post-natal care, and an eye clinic. Apart from a small local hospital, there were very few other medical services for a population of more than two million. The medical need was desperate and the team leader managed to raise a great deal of money to support that work. Some of the team members began to raise some questions about the amount of energy and finance that was being invested in this aspect of our work. Although we were among the newer members of the team, we shared these concerns. We realised that we might not have the full picture of the situation and we wished there were some older and more experienced Christians nearby who could talk us through these issues and give us some wise counsel. Unfortunately, the only other missionary leaders we knew well were 500 miles away in Addis. This was long before the age of instant communications through the Web, and we didn't even have a telephone.

Rosemary and I finally decided reluctantly that since we were not in full agreement with the priorities of the team, we should offer to resign. Our college principal at All Nations Christian College had already warned us that one of the most difficult challenges of being a missionary was getting on with fellow missionaries. We were now discovering that for ourselves. We were very sad about it and I began to feel rather depressed. What we did not know at the time was that I had contracted hepatitis. That probably gave me a "jaundiced" view of the situation!

After sending our resignation back to the UK, we travelled down to Addis Ababa where I was due to take the services at the Anglican church for a month while the chaplain was away. Rosemary planned to do some serious Amharic language study while I looked after the children. After I took the first Communion service, a gynaecologist who had invited us to lunch noticed my yellow eyes and sent me for tests the next day. Once I was diagnosed with hepatitis, I spent much of the next few weeks in bed and Rosemary again had no opportunity to study Amharic.

The walls and bedclothes in the chaplain's vicarage were yellow, which apparently made me look even worse. To complicate matters the water mains outside the vicarage had broken and the only water available was kindly brought to us from the British embassy. The ambassador regularly welcomed us to the embassy to have baths and greeted us with the words, "Here come the dirty Harleys!" Meanwhile, the children, who had seen hippopotamuses once near the Blue Nile Falls, could not pronounce hepatitis properly and went around saying that "Daddy had an optipoptimus in his tummy"!

When we returned to Dabat eight weeks later, we found a letter from the mission in the UK. They had discarded our letter of resignation and expressed the hope that we would continue working in Ethiopia.

When a new leader for the work among the Falasha was appointed, we were asked if we would be willing to go and work in the city of Mek'ele, the capital of Tigray, in order to continue the work that he had been doing there. Our job would be to teach in a school which had more than 1,200 children. Some were as young as five but others were young men in their twenties, who had not been able to attend school earlier. The school had been built by the Ethiopian Orthodox Church primarily to educate and prepare potential priests. Again, this turn of events came as a surprise to us and was not what we had anticipated. Before our arrival in Ethiopia, we were determined not to teach secular subjects in an ordinary school, but now we found ourselves teaching English, modern maths, and even Ethiopian history. On the positive side, we were allowed to teach Religious Education. It was an extraordinary privilege for us as Protestants to be invited to teach the Bible in a school set up for the education of Orthodox priests. As well as teaching, I was asked to serve as principal of the secondary school, which inevitably involved a great deal of administration.

Famine and revolution

There is a great possibility that those who go to serve in another country may be caught up in military conflict or natural disaster. In Ethiopia we encountered both. In 1973, the same year that we moved to Mek'ele, a disastrous famine spread through the northern provinces of Ethiopia, and thousands died of starvation. The failure of Emperor Haile Selassie to handle this crisis contributed to his fall and led to a Marxist revolution. Thousands of refugees from the famine stumbled into Mek'ele from Tigray province seeking food and medical care. I still have a vivid memory of a little girl who had been carried from the Danakil desert to the city. She was four years old and so malnourished that she weighed just eight pounds, the average weight of a newborn baby in the UK.

When pictures of such famine victims were shown on BBC television, Christian Aid, Oxfam, and other NGOs began to help. The German charity, Kindernothilfe, offered to provide funds for school equipment and for the education and care of 200 children orphaned in the famine. I was asked by the local archbishop of the Ethiopian Orthodox Church, Abuna Yohannes, to administer these funds. On one occasion I had a rude shock when the police came to arrest me – I had written cheques that bounced. We soon discovered that there was no money in the bank because the bishop had unwittingly neglected to pay into the bank the huge cheque he had received from abroad. Fortunately, that crisis was soon sorted out, and I was allowed home from the police station.

The archbishop sent me to Asmara, the capital of Eritrea, over 200 miles away, to purchase beds for the 200 orphans to be housed in the school, together with office furniture and school equipment. Once all these things were purchased, I returned to do some teaching, but I was continually interrupted by people seeking admission to the school. All this administration work was not what I was expecting to do. I wanted to be able to spend more time teaching the Bible, both formally in class and informally with the students who came to visit us.

Rosemary and I enjoyed teaching in the Mek'ele school, which was named after Frumentius, who first brought the gospel to Ethiopia. We felt it was a special privilege to teach the Bible to Ethiopian students, some of whom would later become priests. Several of those students expressed an interest in learning about the Bible outside the classroom. They wanted to know more about how they could become committed Christians, and they kept asking me if I could spend more time with them outside school hours looking at the Bible, talking about Jesus, and explaining what it meant to be a Christian. This was the time when the famine was most severe and the administration of the school and the orphanage was so demanding that, much to my regret, I found that I was too busy to be able to spend more time with them. Yet that was what we had come to do.

Teaching in an underground church

We were slowly learning the need to be adaptable, to be ready to change our plans, and to respond to new opportunities. While we were in Begemder, Rosemary and I had conducted regular Bible studies for trainee health workers. Now we were in Mek'ele, Fisseha, one of those health officers, put a group of Christian students and young professionals from the Pentecostal movement in touch with us. They were also keen to have more Bible teaching. Because of the government ban they met each week in a small basement room belonging to another mission and never sang Christian songs to avoid discovery and imprisonment. Their leader had already been imprisoned once for arranging Christian meetings. When we were with them, we were literally in an underground church. It was a privilege for me to teach this group of keen Ethiopian students, and Paul's first letter to the Corinthians, which we studied together, was full of practical advice for young Christians.

There was an embarrassing moment when, in the middle of giving one talk, I was interrupted by an Ethiopian evangelist who had come from Addis Ababa. He told me to sit down. I was speaking from 1 Corinthians 5, which refers to a member of the Corinthian church who was sleeping with his father's wife. Paul urged the church leaders to discipline the man and cast him out of the church, in the hope that he would repent and then could be welcomed back into the fellowship. At this point, the evangelist accused me of wrong teaching. He explained that the church must make a clear stand on this. If anyone went to a prostitute, they could never be welcomed back into the church. The following day, we got together and discussed the issue further. Although I did not agree with his explanation, I could see that immorality was a serious problem in the church and was glad that he felt free to challenge what I said.

On another occasion, visitors from the capital promoted the view that people should not be baptised in the name of the Father, Son, and Holy Spirit, but that baptism should only be in the name of Jesus. Many of the local believers were worried by what they said, but when we looked again at the Gospels, and especially Matthew 28:19, they were reassured that the view of the Jesus-only preachers was unbalanced.

We look back on these times of Bible study with this group of Ethiopian students as being one of the most fruitful times of ministry. We had been surprised how the opportunity arose, since it came from students who were attending a different school from the one where we were teaching. We were about to be surprised again by another unexpected turn of events that would lead us to a totally new chapter in our lives.

We had come to Ethiopia with the expectation of staying for many years, perhaps until we retired. That was our idea, but God had other plans. Unbeknown to us, a letter had already been written from our head office in London, suggesting a totally new direction to our ministry. This letter never arrived, so in blissful ignorance, after four years, we set off on another short home assignment back in the UK. We had a busy speaking schedule, with visits planned to a number of supporting churches, but first we had to meet the new head of CMJ, Walter Barker. That meeting would have a significant impact on our future. The God of the unexpected was about to surprise us again.

Chapter 5

Good News for Jewish People

*In Ethiopia we provided Christians
from some remote locations with Bible
teaching in Amharic on battery-operated
cassette recorders*

Simon Peter answered, "You are the
Messiah, the Son of the living God."

Matthew 16:16

When we met Walter Barker, the general director of CMJ, at the service station near Hungerford on the M4, he asked us what we thought of his letter. We said, "What letter?" Apparently, he had sent us a letter and marked it "Private". This guaranteed that someone would be curious enough to find out what it contained. Not surprisingly, the letter never reached us. Walter explained that the letter contained an invitation for us to leave Ethiopia and return to the UK to lead a small team reaching out in friendship and evangelism to Jewish people in London.

This invitation came as a huge shock and disappointment, especially to Rosemary. We had both spent many years preparing to serve God overseas and we expected that our time in Ethiopia would be our life's work. We had tried our best to learn the language, understand the culture, and build close relationships with people whose customs and way of life were so different from our own. We felt we were only just beginning to find our feet. Surely God, who had guided us so clearly and dramatically to go to Ethiopia, was not calling us to leave so soon.

Rosemary had felt called to mission in Africa from the age of thirteen and she never lost sight of that vision. When I proposed to her on the condition that she would be willing to go anywhere in the world, she took that as confirmation of her own calling. Her desire to read theology at university and teach the Bible in the UK was, in her view, only preparation for a future ministry overseas. The experience in the parish and the year's training at a missionary training college, all seemed to confirm that, in going to Ethiopia, she was going where God was directing. She could not believe it might now be God's will for us to leave Ethiopia after only four or five years in Africa.

Our debt to the Jewish people

Later in the summer, as we were weighing up the unexpected invitation, we attended the annual conference of CMJ. At the conference, we were particularly inspired by Eric Lipson, who having served as a minister of synagogues in Highgate and Sheffield, had come to faith in Jesus as the Jewish Messiah, and been baptised as a Christian. He preferred to describe himself as a Hebrew Christian, though later he adopted the term Messianic Jew. In a moving address, he shared his deep longing that many more Jewish men and women like himself would come to discover the true fulfilment of their faith in Jesus. He challenged the participants to find people who would reach out to the Jewish community and strengthen those who had come to faith in their full identity as both Jews and Christians. As Rosemary and I listened to Eric, we began to wonder if this could be what God was asking us to do.

For a few weeks after the conference, we stayed in a house in London next to my brother and a short distance from the local synagogue. Seeing so many devout Jews walking past our house on the Sabbath reminded us that they are a people whom God has blessed in so many ways and yet who do not understand that God sent his Son to be their Saviour and Messiah. We were asked to return to Ethiopia for at least a year to teach in the Mek'ele school, but we promised to pray about the possibility of moving back to the UK.

Within months of our return to Ethiopia, war broke out between Ethiopia and Eritrea, and, as I mentioned earlier, the border between the two countries was closed. It was now impossible for Andrew to attend the school for missionary children in Asmara.

At the same time, the impact of the Marxist coup that had occurred in Ethiopia in the previous year was being felt among mission communities. The communist government was making it increasingly difficult for missions to continue their work and many missionaries had to leave the country. We knew that it might not be long before this affected the personnel in our own mission. In a year or two we might all be asked to leave the country.

This political climate, together with our memory of the challenge put to us by Eric, made us realise that it might be God's will for us to return to the UK and accept the invitation to work with our mission in the London area. It was not an easy decision, but every indication was that it was the right one. With the assurance that the move was God's will, but with much sadness at the prospect of leaving Ethiopia, we packed our bags and returned to London in the summer of 1975.

Is Jesus the Messiah?

On our return, the first shock we faced was being housed in a large four-bedroom house in Finchley, North London. It was a big change from living in very basic housing in Ethiopia. Initially, we felt rather uncomfortable living in such comparative luxury. Walter Barker, the head of CMJ, explained that our task was to live and witness among the Jewish community of North London which was largely middle-class and relatively wealthy. If we were going to reach out to this community, it was appropriate that we lived among them in housing similar to theirs. The apostle Paul spoke of the need to adapt to the culture and lifestyle of those he sought to reach (1 Corinthians 9:20). It was a new lesson for us to see that sometimes serving God might mean adopting a higher standard of living than we had enjoyed since we were married. We decided we would have to put up with this experience!

I was invited to become an honorary curate at the church where I had served a curacy six years before. This raised the question in the minds of some more humorous friends that perhaps I had made such a bad job of my first curacy that I had been required to repeat it.

When I visited the area bishop to obtain a licence to officiate in the diocese, I was surprised to find that he was reluctant to give me one. "I am good friends with the Chief Rabbi," he explained, "and I don't want you causing any conflict with the Jewish community." I endeavoured to explain that my aim was not to cause conflict but to share the good news in ways that were sensitive and appropriate. This satisfied the bishop sufficiently to grant me a licence, but it was a reminder that many Christians, including those in positions of leadership in the church, regard any form of Christian witness or evangelism among Jewish people as inappropriate. Like many other church leaders, he felt that since Jewish people believe in the same God as Christians and have their own biblical faith that preceded Christianity by almost two millennia, we have no need to share the gospel with them.

Over the next three years, Rosemary and I inevitably became engaged in the debate on whether or not Christians should share their faith with the Jewish people, particularly in the light of the horrendous treatment of Jews by Christians down the centuries. We discovered that many Christians were unaware that Jews had been constantly persecuted by Christians, ridiculed, marginalised, or forced to live in ghettoes. They had never heard how the Crusaders, who went to liberate the Holy Land from Muslim occupation, attacked the Jewish settlements along the Rhine and the Danube, raping and pillaging to raise money for their holy wars. No one had told them the great reformer, Martin Luther, encouraged Christians to attack the Jewish communities and burn their sacred books, nor did they understand the significance of the fact that the rise of the Nazis and the engineering of the Holocaust could originate in a nominally Christian country. In the eyes of most Jewish people, Hitler represents the climax of the Christian maltreatment of Jews, which has continued, almost unabated, since the days of the Roman empire.

Rosemary and I sought to educate Christians about this sad history and to encourage good relationships with local Jewish communities. We recognised the value of dialogue between the church and the synagogue. We believe that in any form of religious dialogue there must be mutual respect and humility, as well as a willingness to learn from one another. There must also be honesty and openness in such dialogue where each party is free to share what they believe.

As we got to know more and more Jewish people in the London area, we came to appreciate their friendship and culture. We appreciated their strong sense of family and community identity; their celebration of biblical religious festivals such as Passover; and their joy of living life to the full. Despite their suffering as Jewish people, the traditional Jewish toast is "L'chaim" – "To life!" I was also impressed by their observance of the Sabbath and their desire to create a unique atmosphere of rest and quietness around the sabbath day that would serve as a foretaste of the joy of heaven.

We looked for opportunities to express our sorrow for what had happened to Jewish people at the hands of Christians. We longed to share with them what we believed about Jesus. We were very aware that Jesus came first as the Messiah of the Jewish nation to fulfil all the promises they had received through the Hebrew Scriptures. As Gentile Christians, we knew we had been invited to share in the rich religious heritage they had enjoyed for thousands of years. The Bible, both the Old and New Testaments, was written almost entirely by Jews, and the Hebrew Scriptures give us our understanding of the character and purposes of God. The challenge we faced was how to repay that debt and share the wonder of knowing Jesus as Saviour and Lord with our Jewish friends.

Soon after we returned to London, I was invited to speak on the subject of evangelism at an international conference in Germany on Jewish–Christian relationships. Among the speakers was Professor Pinchas Lapide, the Jewish New Testament scholar. He had written a book entitled *The Resurrection of Jesus: A Jewish Perspective*,[1] in which he wrote that he accepted the resurrection of Jesus not as an invention of the community of disciples, but as a historic event. He also described Jesus as perhaps the greatest Jew who ever lived and added, with reference to the Christian church, "When Christians show us love, we will listen to their gospel." That was a fair indictment of how the Jewish people have been treated by Christians over nearly 2,000 years. Professor Lapide also said that he regarded Jesus as the Messiah of the Gentiles but not the Messiah of the Jews. To which I replied that if Jesus was the Messiah, he was the Messiah of all.

A year later, Rosemary and I attended a Passover meal in a Jewish home in London. According to custom, an empty place at the table was left for the prophet Elijah who was expected to herald the coming of the Messiah. During the course of the meal, one of the children was sent to open the front door just in case the prophet had arrived, bringing the Messiah with him. At this point, our host turned to us and said, "When the Messiah comes, it will be the first time for us, the second time for you!"

"I have found what my father was looking for"

For more than a hundred years, CMJ's missionaries had lived in various Jewish communities and sought through friendship, acts of kindness, and appropriate witness, to point their neighbours to Jesus the Messiah. It was a ministry that demanded sacrifice and patience, and over the years, a number of Jewish people came to faith.

As these devoted workers continued in their faithful ministry, we began to hear stories of a significant number of Jewish students being brought to faith through the witness of Christian friends. Many of these came from secular homes where there was little or no observance of traditional Jewish customs. Growing up in the 1970s, they were too young to have experienced the Holocaust, which for many Jewish people had made it so difficult to believe in God, let alone Jesus.

Once, I was invited to speak at York University where a Jewish student had recently become a Christian. She was Michelle Guinness, who later worked in broadcasting and who has written a number of bestselling books, including *"Child of the Covenant"*.[2] In that book she explained how as a Jewish girl she rediscovered her roots by finding Christ. She had been brought up to observe all the traditions and ritual of her Jewish culture. An encounter with a Christian raised many questions for her, and she turned to the Bible for the answers.

Before I went to York for the meeting, I was told that two other Jewish students had come to believe in Jesus. By the time I arrived I discovered that another had come to faith. Although this was an exceptional situation, it became evident that on campuses up and down the country Jewish students were becoming Christians. At one point, it seemed that every week one Jewish person was acknowledging Jesus as their Messiah and Lord.

I conducted a survey among 120 Jewish people who had come to faith in Jesus. I asked about their background, the reasons they decided to believe in Jesus as Messiah and Lord, and the difference that faith in Jesus had made to their lives. Most of them came from a liberal or secular background. One came from a family where the only religious festival they observed was Christmas! Almost unanimously, they stated that they came to faith because of what they saw in the lives of Christians around them. One commented, "In Christians I met, I saw people praying to a God who was real and alive to them." Another wrote, "In Christians I saw peace, purpose and the love of God." Only a few came to faith simply through reading the Bible or hearing a sermon.

Most of them experienced opposition from their families when they decided to be baptised. One was completely ostracised by her family who recorded her death in the *Jewish Chronicle*. Painful as it was to be rejected or criticised by their relatives, those who took part in the survey spoke of the impact their new-found faith had on their lives. One said, "At last, I know I am forgiven." Another wrote, "I now know the God of Abraham, Isaac and Jacob." A third made the moving comment, "I have found what my father and grandfather were looking for."

In the church we attended, we met Paul who came from a liberal Jewish home. He had spent a year in hospital and during that time, a Christian school friend visited him every day and chatted with him about what had been going on in school that day. Paul was so impressed by this friend's kindness that he decided to visit his youth club when he got better. As he learned more about the Christian faith and saw the expression of it in his friend's life, Paul decided to become a Christian. He was not sure how his parents would respond to his decision to follow Christ, so he said nothing to them. After a while, his mother began to notice a difference in his behaviour. He was helping with the washing up, making his bed, and keeping his room more tidily. She asked what had happened to him and he explained, somewhat hesitatingly, that he had become a Christian. To his surprise, his mother was delighted because her son was even more thoughtful and helpful than before. Paul's father was less enthusiastic and said he shouldn't be baptised until he was twenty-one. Out of respect for his father, Paul agreed to wait.

Rosemary got to know his mother and took her to a lunch in London, to hear a Jewish lady, Ruth Dobschiner, share her story about how she came to accept Jesus as her Lord and Saviour. Although the primary purpose of the meeting was to invite Jewish guests, the meal they were given consisted of ham and salad. Rosemary could not believe the insensitivity of the organisers. Fortunately, Paul's mother did not keep kosher and was happy to eat ham. She told Rosemary that she had always liked studying the New Testament at school and admired Jesus.

Paul continued to grow in his faith and felt God calling him to be ordained. He went to St John's Nottingham, an Anglican theological college, to prepare for ordination. As part of his course, he was required to serve a placement for a few weeks in a church. When the leaders of the church heard that he had not yet been baptised, they doubted the genuineness of his faith, and explained that they could not accept him. At that point, Paul's father asked him how things were going and Paul explained that there was a problem because he had not been baptised. His father responded with typical Jewish pragmatism, "If this is going to interfere with your chosen career, you had better be baptised."

We remember the day of Paul's baptism well. Both his parents came and they invited all his Christian friends and us to a strawberry and cream tea in their Hampstead home. We were so pleased, not only with the way Paul had grown in his faith, but also with the respect he had shown towards his family. He has since been ordained and served as a minister and evangelist in the UK and Europe. There are very many people who have come to faith through the life and witness of this one Jewish boy, a boy who put his faith in Jesus, the Messiah.

Carmen grew up in Germany before the Second World War. She attended a boarding school where she and another girl were the only two Jews in the whole school. From an early age, she wanted to be an actor and, when there was a school play, she hoped she could play the part of Mary, the mother of Jesus. She was told that she could not play that role because she was a Jew and the Jews killed Jesus! In spite of being treated in this way, Carmen always felt attracted to the Christian faith and believed that she would find meaning and purpose in life in a church.

As her parents saw the rise of anti-Semitism in Germany, they decided to send her to Britain for her own safety. She survived the war but all her family members died in the Holocaust. Even though they had died, along with millions of other Jews, in a nominally Christian country, Carmen still wanted to go to a church. Along with another actor, she began attending All Souls Church in Langham Place, London. She enjoyed the worship but always left before the end of the service to avoid talking to anyone. She was afraid she would experience the same rejection she had experienced elsewhere. However, on one occasion, she was leaving the church early in order to avoid meeting people, but the vicar, Michael Baughen, had also left during the final hymn and met her on the church steps. Carmen apologised for coming because she felt that, as a Jew, she would not be welcome. To which he replied, "Of course you are welcome. It is a privilege to have you here."

That was the first time she had ever heard a Christian say she was welcome in a church, but she soon discovered there were many others at the church who were delighted she was coming. She continued to attend regularly and felt warmly welcomed. It was suggested to her that she might like to meet up with me as someone who had a particular love for the Jewish people. We met for the first time a few weeks later and on many subsequent occasions. She became the dear friend of our whole family and in the course of time, it was my privilege to baptise her.

Messianic Jews

As Rosemary and I saw people like Paul and Carmen coming to faith, we realised God was at work in an exciting way. It was important for our small London team to recognise what God was doing, and to rethink our mission strategy and our changing role in what was taking place. It became evident that our primary ministry in this context was not just evangelism, but educating Christians and churches to reach out to Jewish friends and encouraging the new Jewish believers in their new-found faith. We developed a new strapline for our ministry: "Evangelism, Education, and Encouragement".

The younger generation of those who came to faith often preferred to be called Jewish Christians or Messianic Jews, rather than Hebrew Christians. There were a number of issues to work through about their identity and the maintenance of their Jewish traditions. Sometimes they found the most helpful thing was for them to meet with others who had made the same decision, to be a Jew who believed the Messiah had come.

One of the big issues they faced was which church to join. The services of many churches seemed rather dull compared to the vibrancy of life in the synagogue and the wider Jewish community. Those who had come from a more orthodox background or who had occasionally attended synagogue found it more natural to stand for prayer and to read from a scroll rather than a leather-bound book. They faced a number of other questions. Was there any reason why they shouldn't meet to worship God on Saturday, the Sabbath, rather than on the first day of the week? Could they continue to observe traditional Jewish customs and festivals? One Jewish schoolboy who had been baptised was severely rebuked by his pastor because he attended a celebration of Passover with his family instead of going to the youth Bible study. He was surprised because he knew Jesus celebrated Passover with his disciples and the apostle Paul continued to observe Jewish festivals.

Some of these new believers began to meet together to worship God in a more Jewish style with Hebrew songs and Israeli dancing. Some formed their own Messianic congregations as a cultural expression of their faith, although they were keen to avoid a new kind of legalism or appearing to be separating themselves from Gentile believers.

In 1979, I was involved in the formation of the Lausanne Consultation on Jewish Evangelism (LCJE). The Lausanne movement was founded by Dr Billy Graham at a conference held in Lausanne, Switzerland, in 1974. It rapidly grew into a global movement that inspired evangelical leaders to collaborate for world evangelisation. It organised a second conference in Pattaya, Thailand, at which I was asked to be involved in the mini-consultation on ministry among the Jewish communities around the world. My responsibility was to coordinate the reports of more than twenty groups of people engaged in different kinds of Jewish ministry. These groups represented a wide spectrum of Jewish mission agencies. A group of eighteen mission leaders and theological consultants then met for ten days in Pattaya to discuss those reports and produce a booklet entitled *Christian Witness to the Jewish People*.[3]

Those who attended this consultation were struck by the warmth of fellowship and sense of common purpose within the group, in spite of the different theological, and particularly millennial, perspectives. There was a strong desire not to lose this sense of fellowship and cooperation, so it was agreed, over a few cups of coffee, that out of this group a permanent fellowship should be set up. Since they did not want LCJE to be dominated by one of the big mission agencies on either side of the Atlantic, I was asked if I would be willing to serve as the first international facilitator.[4]

Among those who were particularly influential in helping this fellowship of Jewish agencies to succeed were Moishe Rosen and Susan Perlmann of Jews for Jesus (JFJ), who invested a great deal into the group. Others who played a leading role were the Revd Murdo MacLeod, director of Christian Witness to Israel, and the Revd Ole Kvarme, who worked for ten years in Israel and later became Bishop of Oslo.

This group continues to the present time, and has resulted in an amazing level of cooperation between agencies, although they differ widely in their doctrinal position and methodology. These agencies came together because of their desire to share the good news with Jewish people and their recognition that they could do more together than by themselves. I served for ten years as the first international coordinator of LCJE and was responsible for organising the early conferences.

Some Christians argue that God has abandoned the Jewish people and chosen the church to fulfil his purposes for the world. The apostle Paul, however, contends that God has never, and could never, abandon his chosen people "for God's gifts and his call are irrevocable" (Romans 11:29). Paul sees evidence for the ongoing purposes of God for the Jewish people in the fact that so many of the first followers of Jesus, including himself, were Jewish. "Did God reject his people? By no means!" Paul argues. "I am an Israelite myself, a descendant of Abraham, from the tribe of Benjamin" (Romans 11:1). In the past sixty years, more Jewish people have come to believe that Jesus is their Messiah, Saviour, and Lord than ever before. By the mid-1970s, according to *Time* magazine, the number of Messianic Jews or Jewish Christians in the US was over 50,000. By 1993, this number had grown to 160,000 in the US and about 350,000 worldwide. Today, it is estimated that there are over 400 Messianic synagogues worldwide, with at least 150 in the US.

It is important to note that these Messianic Jews do not consider that they have been converted to another religion. Rather, they maintain that their faith is now completed for they are Jews who know the Messiah has come. They consider themselves both Jewish and Christian. They have much to share with us and teach us. They can increase our understanding of the Old Testament and explain the significance of key terms of the New Testament, like sacrifice, atonement, redemption, and Messiah. They can help us appreciate the significance of the Jewish customs and festivals, such as Passover and Pentecost.

Jewish Christians also face the challenge of sharing their Messianic faith with friends and relatives. We need to uphold them in prayer as they often face criticism or rejection from family members because of their new-found faith. At the same time, we rejoice with them that they have found the true shepherd who came to seek and save the lost sheep of the house of Israel (Matthew 15:24).

Rosemary and I greatly enjoyed those years in North London, seeing God at work and spending time with Jewish friends who had come to faith in Jesus. We loved our house, which proved big enough to provide a place for them to meet together. We were pleased that the children could attend a local primary school and didn't have to go to a boarding school at a very young age. Catherine, our youngest, was only three when we returned to the UK and she was sad to leave her cat behind in Ethiopia. She was especially thrilled when a stray cat wandered into our house and made itself at home. A short while later, Rosemary's mother, who was staying with us, was not so thrilled when the cat decided to have kittens underneath our dining table one Saturday lunchtime!

We happily settled as a family in North London, expecting to be there for some years, but towards the end of our third year, we had an unexpected phone call.

Chapter 6

To All Nations

Dr Richard Harvey,
Senior Researcher, Jews for Jesus

*And the things you have heard me say in the
presence of many witnesses entrust to reliable
people who will also be qualified to teach others.*

2 Timothy 2:2

By 1978, Rosemary and I had been working in London for almost three years, visiting churches and encouraging the growing number of young Jewish Christians, when we received a phone call from David Morris, the principal of the college where we had trained before going to Ethiopia. He asked if we would like to explore the possibility of joining the staff of All Nations Christian College (ANCC). We had gone to Africa with the hope of being able to teach in a Bible college, but we had never considered that one day we might teach in one in the UK. I took the phone call and immediately pointed out that Rosemary was more qualified to teach theology than I was. To which David Morris replied, "Well, it's really Rosemary we want. We will have to take you as well!"

All Nations is set in the beautiful Easneye estate on a small hill overlooking the Lea Valley in Hertfordshire. The main house, built by the Buxton family in 1869, is surrounded by lawns, gardens and woodlands, carpeted with daffodils in early spring, followed by bluebells. Students are often surprised by the pheasants, deer, and variety of birds found in the grounds. It would be hard to find a more pleasant environment in which to work.

The house was built by John Buxton, son of Sir Thomas Fowell Buxton, who worked with William Wilberforce for the abolition of the slave trade. The Buxtons were deeply committed to Christ and used to gather daily for prayer in the main entrance hall together with all their servants. Many members of the family and several of the servants became missionaries. In 1869, when the family took possession of the property, Hannah Buxton, Sir Thomas's widow, expressed the wish that the house would always "be inhabited by faithful servants of God in and through Christ Jesus, and that it may ever be a habitation of God in the hearts of the inhabitants by the Holy Spirit, and Christ be honoured, confessed and served, and this place be a fountain of blessing in the church and to the world". Ninety-four years later, in 1963, an agreement was reached between the Buxton family and the college council for the house to become the new home of what was then called All Nations Missionary College.

College ethos

Having studied at the College before we went to Africa, Rosemary and I were familiar with its ethos and fully agreed with David Morris's understanding of mission in the post-colonial era and with the pattern of holistic training he had developed. This was borne out of his personal experience as a missionary in Nigeria during its final years as a British colony.

David Morris had witnessed the arrogance of Western missionaries at first hand and was convinced a radical change was necessary in the attitude of Western missionaries. He had observed that some had an exalted picture of themselves, their gifts, and what they were going to achieve. They often showed an inability to appreciate the culture and religion of the people among whom they served. Morris was determined to develop a programme of practical and relevant training, where the students learned how to live, work, and witness appropriately among the people they hoped to serve. Rosemary and I knew how much we had appreciated the year we spent at the college before going to Ethiopia and how much we had benefitted from such a well-rounded pattern of training. We especially realised the value of the practical courses we attended and the advice we were given on living in a remote part of the world, learning a new language, adapting to a simpler lifestyle, and keeping well in a tropical climate.

Morris saw the need to focus on a student's personal relationship with Jesus and their character, which was also an important part of their witness to the gospel they preached. Spiritual maturity and proven ability were clearly emphasized in the early church and Morris was convinced that they should be given priority in any training programme. He knew that if there were no dynamic personal faith, no evidence of a personal relationship with Jesus, the words these missionaries shared would sound hollow and unconvincing.

The tutorial system Morris developed also helped foster students' personal relationship with Christ. As tutors, we were not just academic advisers, but also pastors, counsellors, and friends. Although the staff were expected to devote a great deal of time to this interaction with students, with group worship three times a week, occasional informal meals and regular one-to-one meetings, we quickly learned to appreciate the way it enabled us to provide counsel and encouragement at a deeper and more personal level. We also discovered that our lives were enriched by the faith and commitment of the men and women in our group.

It was also our realisation that, in the goodness of God, we had had a variety of ministry experience over a relatively short period of time. This helped us in our role as tutors to counsel and encourage those who were anticipating serving in very different ministries. We had been involved together in church and youth ministry in the UK. We had worked both in rural and urban ministry in Africa. We had encountered the tension of being engaged in both social action and evangelism, and experienced the challenges of ministering to a specific religious community. We saw how God had prepared us for these new roles and we subsequently enjoyed many very happy and fulfilling years of teaching and, subsequently, leading the college.

Serving God together

Rosemary and I always wanted to serve together in ministry. We had both studied theology and wanted to be involved in missionary service and in Bible teaching. During the three years we worked at Christ Church, North Finchley, we both were engaged in working among teenagers and young adults. In Ethiopia, we shared the leadership of Bible studies in our home. In London, we hosted many young Jewish Christians for meals and times of fellowship. We were especially pleased to join ANCC because, now all the children were at school, it meant we would have more opportunities to teach and work together.

David Morris was a leader who recognised the gifts and experience of the women on the staff and wanted them to play an equal role in training both male and female students. Unusually for the time he was very happy for women to teach from the Scriptures. This made it possible for us, as a couple, to be engaged together for many years in the same ministry, using our different gifts. Rosemary taught some New Testament, lectured on New Religious Movements and Theological Education by Extension, and organised seminars on the History of Mission and leading group Bible studies. I focused mainly on the Old Testament and preparing some students for the Cambridge Diploma in Religious Studies.

Sadly, in our subsequent ministry, we did not always find the same positive attitude towards the use of Rosemary's gifts. There were times when, despite her having several theological degrees, many years' experience in ministry and a gift of teaching, she was not invited to teach, while less mature men with no experience or training were invited to do so. Once, when we were both invited to speak at the Oxford Christian Union, the newly elected president was shocked when he realised we had both been invited and intended to speak from the set biblical passage. We carried on as planned, however! One of our female colleagues at All Nations, Ruth Geisner, recalls how she was invited to speak at one university Christian Union, only to receive a letter a week or so before she was due to speak. The committee of the CU had noticed that she was a woman and, therefore, she would not be allowed to expound scripture but could share from her mission experience in Africa.

ANCC had married couples who worked together in teaching and providing pastoral care. There were also several single women on the staff. Since ANCC had been formed by the merger of two women's colleges and one men's college, the principal determined to maintain parity between the number of male and female lecturers on the faculty. This was a progressive policy for an evangelical college, especially at a time when there were relatively few women theological lecturers in Britain. When the three colleges merged, the leadership was shared between David Morris, as principal, and Meg Foote, who had served as principal of Mt Hermon Missionary Training College, as vice-principal.

One student, who came from a church which did not allow women to teach or exercise leadership, asked to have a male tutor for both first and second years, but was not allowed to do so. The policy of the college was clear. Students who chose to come to ANCC had to be willing to be taught by women.

The role of women in ministry was also underlined by the requirement that all wives would be involved in the training course at the college. Both David Morris and Meg Foote were convinced that in the second half of the twentieth century husbands and wives should prepare together for cross-cultural ministry. In previous decades, men and women had been encouraged by some agencies to go overseas single and only marry after their first term of service, often a period of four or five years! Morris argued that wives should always be seen as partners in mission and should have the same opportunity to prepare. In consequence, married couples were accepted for training only if both husband and wife were full-time students. Both had to attend lectures and were expected to complete assignments and do some practical courses. A nursery was set up in the college so that children could be looked after in the mornings, while their parents were attending lectures.

Looking at the Bible through other eyes

When I first joined the staff, I was thrilled to be given sixty hours of lectures each year in which to expound the first five books of the Bible. It was a joy to be able to spend so much time looking at the biblical text, although it took a lot of time to prepare and make extensive notes for lectures, before the days of computers. On one occasion, Rosemary went back to the college in the evening and agreed to bring home my large file of handwritten notes on Genesis. When she arrived home, she didn't have them. Then she remembered she had put them on the top of our car but had forgotten to put them inside before she drove off. We went back towards the college and found the sheets of notes, more than 100 pages, scattered on the roadside and all over a ploughed field. I know we are commanded to spread the word but I don't think this is what was intended! In the event, we recovered every single page, and marital harmony was maintained.

As I developed these courses, I realised it was important not only to study the text, but also to examine how to teach and explain each passage in a different cultural context. How do you relate, for example, biblical teaching about the character of God as revealed in the first chapter of Genesis to the understanding of God found in traditional religion, Islam, or Hinduism?

Genesis opens with the clear statement that there is only one omnipotent God who created the world. Judaism and Islam share this conviction but do not accept the concept of the Trinity, which Christians see as being reflected through scripture. Other religions speak of many gods or a hierarchy of gods and spirits, whereas some world views reject any idea of a supreme creator. Anyone who wishes to share the good news of Jesus has to understand those they are seeking to reach and build a bridge between their world view and biblical teaching.

Many ancient cultures have traditional stories that record a time when God lived in close harmony with men and women until they acted in defiance of God and drove him away. In their view, now this supreme God is far away, it is no longer possible for humans to relate to him. In the past, some missionaries have been unaware of these traditional stories or have dismissed them out of hand. In my lectures, I sought to encourage students to think about how they would relate biblical truth to legends of the fall or how they would explain the doctrine of the Trinity to monotheists.

Students would often enrich the lectures by sharing their own cultural observations. One student from a nomadic tribe in Kenya told us how he had become a Christian through reading the genealogy of Jesus in Matthew's Gospel. He explained that in his culture, the first thing a mother teaches her son is the names of his ancestors, starting with his father, grandfather, great-grandfather, and so on. This gave the child a sense of identity. So, when he read the genealogy of Jesus, he realised that Jesus was a real historical person, and the New Testament was true and not a fairy story made up by Westerners.

Whereas Western students found it difficult to relate to a book like Leviticus with its constant reference to sacrifice and the shedding of blood, many from other parts of the world found that the practices described in Leviticus were similar to those in their own culture. This not only enabled them to understand parts of the Old Testament that seemed strange to Western students, but also gave them a greater appreciation of New Testament passages that describe the death of Jesus in terms of sacrifice. Peter Lomongin from Uganda, who later became the Anglican bishop of Karamoja, explained that cattle, as well as goats, sheep, and camels, play a vital role in the life and culture of the Karamojong. They are highly dependent on their livestock for survival and their diet is comprised mostly of milk and occasionally blood from their cows. He went on to explain that his people used to mark all their cattle and tents with blood as a sign of purification.

It was fascinating to see which books of the Bible were particularly popular in which country. Students from Ethiopia appreciated the book of Proverbs because the quoting of proverbs was so popular in their culture. Those who had worked or lived in China commented on the value of Ecclesiastes as an evangelistic tool in China because it resonated with many who felt that life was meaningless.

The staff

On one Monday, David Morris came into the communal time of college worship, carrying an "L" plate, the sign that is used in the UK to indicate learner drivers. "Whether we are staff or students, we are all learners, and we should all go on learning for the whole of our lives," he explained. "Throughout your working lives, never give up on learning. Never think you have arrived and know it all. Those of us who are tutors still have so much to learn, and we learn a great deal from you as students. Whether we are staff or students, trainers or trainees, we are learning together – all fellow disciples of the Lord Jesus, fellow-pilgrims, encouraging, challenging and supporting each other."

His words reflect the ethos of the college better than anything else could. Rosemary and I enjoyed teaching in a college where you were not expected to have all the answers or to present a picture of a permanently victorious Christian life. We learned so much from the students and have been encouraged by the continuing fellowship we have had with them. We were invited to visit many in different parts of the world and are now enjoying those who drop in for a break on their way to holidays in Devon and Cornwall. We also benefitted so much from our colleagues. It may seem invidious to name any, for all contributed to a harmonious team in an extremely effective programme, yet there were some who fulfilled a particularly significant role during our time at the college.

Meg Foote, as vice-principal, shared David Morris's vision for the united college and worked closely with him for the realisation of that vision. Her wise and measured counsel often served as the ideal antidote to his more imaginative ideas and occasionally bizarre sense of humour. John Syratt, who joined the college in 1973, brought his considerable expertise as the chief accountant of a retail grocery chain. He managed to put the college on a more secure financial footing, and was the quiet influence who helped the whole organisation run efficiently. When David Morris, who had frequently suffered bouts of depression, was no longer able to continue as principal, Meg Foote took over as acting principal along with Ron Davies, the director, until New Zealander Dr Ray Windsor became principal in 1982. He had worked as a heart surgeon in India for many years before becoming international director of Interserve. In his relatively short time as principal, Ray encouraged a shift from an Oxbridge-based learning style, which focused on the writing of long assignments, to one that was more prevalent in the United States, which laid an equal emphasis on book reviews and short writing projects. We found these shorter assignments gave the students the opportunity to think through a wider variety of topics relating to their future work. We also appreciated Ray's warm personality and the pastoral care he gave staff and students. At the same time, we realised it was a new experience for him to work in a college like All Nations and adapt to British culture.

David Morris had built up a team of tutors with a wide variety of experience and expertise in mission. Martin Goldsmith and his wife, Elizabeth, had worked for many years in Southeast Asia with OMF. They wrote numerous books and Martin had an amazing gift of communication. We always said that he didn't need visual aids, because his face was a visual aid. He would sometimes make an outrageous remark during a lecture and then show on his face absolute shock and horror at the very idea he had just expressed.

Bob Hunt and Ruth Geisner oversaw the practical church experience of students. They had both served in Africa. Margaret Jones and Jan Stafford led the pastoral courses and their personal counselling and care of students were much appreciated. Stan Bruce taught biblical languages and was a superb librarian who transformed the college collection of books. Later, many other staff joined us, bringing their experience from different parts of the world, including Chris and Liz Wright. They spent a year at the college while they waited for visas to teach at Union Biblical Seminary in India and subsequently returned to join the staff on a permanent basis. Chris became academic dean and followed me as principal.

Then there was Tom Paget, who had been on the staff since the early days of David Morris. He had oversight of the college grounds and the practical courses. He loved telling the students what to do. He seemed to get particular pleasure out of making the doctors and other highly qualified students perform the most menial tasks like cleaning the toilets or clearing the drains! When we were students, I remember being given mundane tasks in the garden, not my favourite thing. Despite the way Tom loved bossing us all about, everybody loved him!

There were many others too who contributed so much – the catering staff, the administrative staff, those who supervised accommodation for married couples, and those who ran the nursery and the bookshop. There was no sense of hierarchy. We were a family, all seeking to serve the Lord together. Rosemary and I so enjoyed working in such a harmonious and talented team. It was a very special place to work.

The students

During the fifteen years we spent at the college, we were blessed not only by our colleagues, but also by the gifted and dedicated students who came from all over the world to spend one or two years preparing for the work to which God was calling them. Many had already been involved in ministry in their own country or abroad. They had struggled with the challenges of cross-cultural mission in the modern world and came with their own questions and insights. The college had trebled in size from the time we were students eight years before. Many more were coming from Europe and farther afield. It was an amazing mix of people, who brought a variety of gifts from diverse backgrounds, denominations, and cultures.

While more than half of the students came from the medical and teaching professions,[1] others came from a wide spectrum of professions and occupations, ranging from solicitor to secretary, agriculturalist to architect, blacksmith to banker, chemist to carpenter, pilot to plumber, confectioner to computer programmer. One was a farmer who felt called to reach the farming communities of East Anglia. Another was a car mechanic, who was able to use his maintenance skills in a diocese in East Africa, while his wife used her gifts as a nurse. One student, who had grown up in a nomadic community in Africa, was not used to writing assignments, but she appreciated the lectures and took an active part in discussions.

One of the challenges we faced as tutors was in knowing which applicants to accept. Along with other staff members, we would spend an hour or more interviewing prospective students, trying to assess their call and the suitability of the college course for them. We required three references from each applicant and sometimes it was the reference from their secular employer that was most revealing. On one occasion, the secular referee had drawn a line through the questions that asked about the candidate's Christian faith. "I do not understand these questions," he wrote, "but if this person is a Christian, I wish all my employees were Christians." This is a great example of the impact a Christian can make in the secular world, and a reminder that those who by their lives are consistent witnesses for Christ, while working in their own country, are likely to be effective witnesses when they serve overseas.

Students from the UK

Inevitably, in a community of nearly 200 students, we spent more time with some than others, either because they were in our tutor group or because we shared a common interest. The few I mention here only represent a fraction of the 1,500 students who studied at the college during the time we were on the staff but, hopefully, they give some idea of those who came to college and the ministries in which they were engaged after they left.

Richard Harvey had grown up in a liberal Jewish home. He came to believe in Jesus as the Messiah while he was in the sixth form at school. Studying theology at university, he experienced tension between his academic studies and his deep personal faith in Jesus. It was as though he had these in separate compartments in his mind, and it took some time before he could harmonise the two to his own satisfaction. He was very conscious of his Jewish identity and when he applied to come to ANCC to prepare for future ministry, he described himself as a Messianic Jew rather than a Christian. Motivated by a deep concern for his own people, he subsequently served with Jewish mission agencies, including CMJ and JFJ. After he completed a PhD at Birmingham University on Messianic Jewish theology under Rabbi Professor Dan Cohn-Sherbrook, he returned to the college to join the staff and open the students' eyes to a Jewish understanding of the Hebrew Scriptures. Later, his passion to share the good news with his fellow Jews led him back to ministry with JFJ, both as an evangelist and as their in-house theologian.

Peter was a doctor who ambitiously, and on that occasion unsuccessfully, attempted to complete his Membership of the Royal Colleges of Physicians examination whilst studying at All Nations. Peter and his wife Alison went on to serve for seven years at the Nazareth Hospital, Israel, and he subsequently became Professor of Clinical Genetics at Exeter University, while Alison joined the hospital chaplaincy team as a volunteer. Another doctor, also called Peter, came from New Zealand and, and after working as a surgeon, served as Chief Executive of the Christian Medical Fellowship in the UK for twenty-seven years, often appearing in the media presenting a biblical perspective on ethical issues.

Roger and Jane are a couple who had a strong call to mission overseas. Although Roger had a PhD in chemistry and good career prospects, they laid this aside and came to the college to prepare together for their future ministry. They felt that OMF was the mission with which they would like to serve, and towards the end of their second year, they made a formal application to OMF. They were shocked when their application was rejected on the grounds of Jane's mental health. Feeling disappointed and confused, they became involved in the ministry of a local church. A year later, the decision was reversed and they were accepted for service with OMF. Over the next thirty years, they served as missionaries in four Asian countries, training theological students and pastors. Their story serves as a reminder that God will guide those who seek to follow him and that setbacks may only be temporary.

Students from overseas

Over the years, ANCC became a truly international college, to a point where overseas students constituted more than half the student body. A doctor from Malaysia had qualified in the UK but was determined to serve in his own country. He felt the Lord wanted him to serve in East Malaysia, although the career prospects were less promising than in the more prosperous West Malaysia. During his time in the UK, he had initiated the Malaysian Christian Fellowship. On his return home, he played a leading role in one church before starting a new church in a five-star hotel in Kota Kinabalu in East Malaysia. The church grew exponentially and reached a new and significant section of the community.

A Brazilian couple, Silas and Marcia, brought with them their own vivacity and passion for world mission. On her first day at ANCC, Marcia expressed her surprise that I was leading the college. She told me, "David, you are too young to be the principal!" In 1975, her father had founded Brazil's first interdenominational and national mission organization. Silas and Marcia eventually took over the leadership of the mission, which currently has ninety-two Brazilian missionaries serving in nineteen countries. They continue to play a significant role in training other Brazilians for mission.

A keen footballer from North Africa became a key leader in the growth of the church and the missionary movement in his own country. Before coming to ANCC, he had trained as a football coach and helped prepare the national team for the Seoul Olympics. When he returned to North Africa, he and his Chinese wife, whom he met at All Nations, worked with Operation Mobilization. They established the first residential centre to train his own people for cross-cultural mission in North Africa and the Middle East. The indigenous church has witnessed huge growth in recent decades, especially among Muslims coming from a Berber background.

From all nations to all nations

Whereas other Bible colleges offered training for pastoral work or evangelism in the home country, the distinct focus of ANCC was to train men and women for cross-cultural ministry. Consequently, students were only accepted if they had a strong sense of a call to this kind of ministry. Some had already applied to, or were in conversation with, a missionary society, while others had come to the college as accepted candidates, as we had done in 1969. Others were undecided about their future field of service, but as they gained a clearer understanding of the needs and opportunities in different parts of the world, together with a more realistic assessment of their own gifts, they were better able to decide on the way forward.

Complete statistics are not available on where the students eventually went, but their anticipated field of service, recorded when they first came to the college, gives some indication of where they hoped to go. In 1980, more than half the student population were interested in serving in Asia, while a quarter felt called to Africa. About 10 per cent were considering service in Europe, while some were preparing to serve in Latin America or the Middle East.

Several of the most popular destinations were those having close historic ties with Britain (India, Nigeria, Ghana, Pakistan, Malaysia) or with another colonial power (Rwanda, Indonesia, Brazil). In the case of Thailand, Ethiopia, and Nepal there was no such historic association, but each of these countries presented considerable scope for missionary service. A further important factor in the choice of a field of service lay in the image of the various missionary agencies. Agencies that produced attractive publicity and communicated an approach to mission that coincided with that held by the students, inevitably attracted more applications. Societies like Wycliffe Bible Translators, OMF, and Interserve became increasingly popular. They recommended and, in some cases, insisted that their candidates had at least a year of residential preparation.

Many students used their professional skills and qualifications to serve local communities and aid development in the nations to which they went. This was not only a practical way of demonstrating the love of God, it was in many cases the only way they could enter the countries, which had closed their borders to missionaries. Those who were in the medical profession served as surgeons, doctors, nurses, physiotherapists, and occupational therapists. Some worked in remote rural communities, bringing medical aid where none had previously existed. Others were engaged in training medical staff, lecturing in universities, or undertaking medical research. There were those who specialised in particular fields, such as leprosy, AIDS, or ministry to the visually impaired, whereas others were involved in palliative care.

Responding to specific needs, some worked among prostitutes, orphans, and the homeless. Others were engaged in community development or projects to bring electricity or improved sanitation. Some, motivated by a growing awareness of the impact of climate change, joined agencies with a strong focus on the protection of the environment.

Increasingly the ministry in which these people worked was undertaken at the request of and under the leadership of the local church or community. So, where the church grew in maturity, those who came to serve did so under national leadership. The role of the missionary was changing. Some were invited to train pastors or help in the development of youth work. Some of those who had come to All Nations returned to their own countries to engage in training their own people to be missionaries.

Some students had a particular burden for reaching those who had never heard about Jesus. Others were called to be involved in Bible translation, bringing the Word of God to people in their own mother tongue. Several of the students from Africa returned to continue their work with Scripture Union. Other Africans had already been ordained and returned to responsible positions in their home church. Several became bishops, including Andrew Adano, who was subsequently consecrated as the first Anglican bishop in Kenya from a nomadic background. Tragically, he died with senior government officials when the police helicopter in which they were travelling crashed just outside Marsabit, in Northern Kenya in 1996.

After years of service, many of the former students were given responsibilities of leadership in mission agencies or NGOs. Most of the students were twenty-five or older when they came to college but among the younger students were Ian and Anne-Marie, who had been involved with the Christian Union at Cambridge and brought a party of students to visit ANCC. After they completed their degrees, Ian took a secular job for a year, but Martin Goldsmith, who knew them well, felt they should not delay coming to college any longer. In spite of their young age and relative inexperience in the secular world, they were accepted as students in the college for the two-year course. After leaving the college, they served as church planters in the Philippines before Ian was appointed in his thirties as one of the five international directors of OMF International. When I later served as general director of OMF, he served as international director for evangelism. Once his term of service in that role was completed, Ian and Anne-Marie started all over again by going to a completely new country in East Asia, using their experience to lead the team there. In 2020, they returned to the UK to be involved in diaspora ministry – that is, ministry among Asians living and studying in Britain.

A mature couple who came to study at college were both lawyers from Arkansas in the USA. On completing their course, they went to serve with Wycliffe in Tanzania. They returned to the USA to settle their younger daughter in university but very soon, and much to their surprise, the husband was appointed as US ambassador to Tanzania by President Clinton. Once they got over the shock, they settled down to their new job but, coming from a teetotal background, they struggled a bit with the choice of wines for embassy dinners!

Many single women who studied at ANCC went on to play significant roles in the places where they served. One taught in a mission training centre in Brazil; another taught in a theological college for Orthodox priests in Ethiopia before being ordained as an Anglican; another worked among the poor and deprived in Peru; while yet another worked among prostitutes in Taiwan. One woman from Zimbabwe played a leading role in the Girl Guide movement in the UK.

Global perspectives

One factor that influenced the choices students made about their future ministry was the input of visiting lecturers. The practice of having a visiting lecturer in residence for a term every year was introduced by Ray Windsor. He invited Asian leaders, whom he had known during his work in that continent, to come and share their perspectives and experience. Among these were Dr P. T. Chandapilla, the Vicar General of St Thomas Evangelical Church of India. He ministered to the university students in India and the church at large through new mission initiatives, including the founding of Jubilee Memorial Bible College at Chennai. Although he was so widely recognised and admired in his own country, what struck me was his humility and simplicity of lifestyle. Someone remarked that "he lives like Mother Teresa, but thinks like Jean Calvin". When he preached at the college services, he did not try to impress us with his academic knowledge, but spoke with a gentleness and sincerity, which reflected the reality of his relationship with Christ. He enjoyed his time with us, but complained about the English weather, since it rained every day during the summer term, and only stopped on the day he was due to leave! Another visitor from India was P. S. Thomas, who was assistant general secretary of the Indian Evangelical Mission (IEM), one of the largest indigenous missions in India. He shared how his experience of failing as a missionary in his first term of service[2] helped him understand the vital importance of training those who are preparing for cross-cultural ministry. This enabled him to play a leading role in training new candidates for mission service in his own mission. His wife was pleased that their time at ANCC proved to be a real sabbatical, because he had shed his responsibilities for a term and was able to spend the time chatting with students and watching cricket.

Other visiting lecturers included David Lee from South Korea and Joshua Ogawa from Japan. Dr Lee played a leading role in the emergence of the missionary movement in Korea, founding the Global Missionary Fellowship and serving as director of the Global Missionary Training Center in Seoul. He made a significant contribution to the global missionary movement and became chairman of the World Evangelical Alliance Mission Commission (WEAMC). Joshua Ogawa and his wife had served as missionaries in Indonesia. He shared with the students that they found it very hard to be missionaries in that country because of the experiences people had endured during the Second World War at the hands of the Japanese. They saw little fruit until the day when their eighteen-month-old daughter died. When the local people saw how they reacted to their loss and observed their confidence that their child was now in heaven, they started to ask questions about the Christian faith. Their bereavement unlocked the door of that village to the gospel.

These visitors, coming from all over the world, shared from their vast experience in mission and mission training. They made a huge impact on staff and students, broadening our horizons, and enabling us to learn from their insights and see the world of mission through their eyes. They served as a reminder of the increasing role in world mission that was being played by Christians from the majority world.[3]

Chapter 7

College Principal

David, Bishop John Taylor and Dr John Stott
at ANCC for the launch of the MA programme
in 1992

*"Be strong and courageous. Do not be afraid;
do not be discouraged, for the Lord your God
will be with you wherever you go."*

Joshua 1:9

When Joshua was tasked to succeed Moses as the leader of the people of Israel, he felt totally inadequate for the job. He was acutely aware of his own limitations. Joshua was much younger than Moses and without his privileged background and education. He had not experienced a dramatic call like Moses received at the burning bush, nor had he spent many weeks in the presence of God on Mount Sinai. It was one thing to stand beside Moses and observe him leading the people through the wilderness, teaching them the Word of God and performing miracles. It was quite another to step into Moses' shoes and lead the people of God into the Promised Land. Small wonder that Joshua felt nervous and had to be exhorted time and again to be strong and of good courage.

When I was asked by the college council to become the next principal of All Nations and to continue the development of the excellent training programme David Morris had established, I understood how Joshua felt. I certainly was not expecting to be invited to fulfil this role. Rosemary and I had been at the college for six years – I was the vice-principal by then – and we were wondering whether we should move on. Although we loved teaching there, we realised our own experience of mission was receding into the background. We questioned if the teaching we gave and the examples we cited would still be relevant in a rapidly changing world.

A few months before I received the invitation to be principal, I was approached by two churches asking if I would be interested in becoming their vicar. One of these churches was thirty miles away and it would have meant the children changing schools. Andrew would have been in the middle of A-levels and Ruth her O-levels. The other church was close by and would have caused less interruption in the life of the family. I went to talk things over with Ray Windsor, who had taken over as principal from David Morris two years before. Much to my surprise, he said he was going to have to return to New Zealand and expressed the hope that I would succeed him. A few months later, I received the formal invitation from the college council to become the principal.

I was encouraged by the staff's support for my appointment, and was very grateful to inherit the gifted team who had worked together so harmoniously under David Morris and Ray Windsor. I was also aware I had little experience of leadership at this level: I lacked Ray Windsor's experience and David's winsome and dynamic personality. There were many lessons I needed to learn about leadership, and time alone would tell how successfully I learned them. As far as I was able, I determined to follow the examples of my predecessors and to emulate their style of leadership.

Maintaining a harmonious team

One observation I had made was the careful and prayerful way in which David Morris slowly built up his staff team. He looked for people with pastoral gifts, who would work well in a team and relate easily to others. One of his pet phrases was, "we need 'people persons'." He expected the staff to be mature and committed Christians, with mission experience, good qualifications, and the gift of communication. But first and foremost, they had to be approachable. They had to have the ability to relate with ease both to their fellow members of staff and to the students.

I also noticed the respect David Morris had for every member of the staff, whether they were tutors, accountants, secretaries, cooks, or librarians. He involved us all, whatever our role, in the weekly staff and prayer meetings, and only made major decisions about college policy after the widest consultation. He wanted all the staff to be happy about the methods and aims of the college. He insisted that student references, sent out in the name of the college, were approved at the plenary staff meeting and that new staff members were vetted by the whole staff. He made it his business to know how each member of staff was getting on. He would spend several hours each week just walking around the college, visiting staff in their office, study, or place of work. It was a principle he first learned in the army, where he had begun to understand the importance of a good relationship between an officer and his troops.

I resonated with David's philosophy that every Christian is valuable in the eyes of God and each makes a distinctive contribution to the community. I continued the practice of inviting all staff members, whatever their role in college, to attend the weekly staff meeting. I made a point of spending time with each member of staff, showing interest in them, their work, their families, and their perspectives on the running of the college. In subsequent leadership roles, notably when I was dean of Discipleship Training Centre in Singapore and general director of OMF International, I sought to maintain a similar practice of leadership.

Making decisions together

Over the years, Rosemary and I had observed a wide variety of leadership styles. On the one hand, we noticed that some pastors were autocratic and tended to make all-important decisions affecting their church by themselves without any consultation. On the other hand, we saw some church leaders who were so afraid of their elders or council that they made no decisions at all and provided no vision for the development of the church. We had already seen how Morris built an amazingly harmonious team of gifted and strong-willed personalities by consulting them on all major issues. When he retired, Meg Foote and then Ray Windsor continued to provide good pastoral care for both staff and students and made decisions by consensus.

During Ray's time, the college was unexpectedly left a large amount of money by an elderly lady who had visited shortly before her death and discussed the possibility of leaving part of her estate to ANCC. This proved very timely because the college was growing. Some years there were nearly a thousand applications for 100 places. The problem was the college was now bursting at the seams and the dining room was far too small. There was an urgent need to build a new larger dining room. A staff meeting was held to discuss where it should be built. After a lengthy discussion, Ray concluded with general agreement, that the dining room should be located in the former stable yard. However, after the meeting ended, it became apparent that a number of the staff were concerned that we had reached the decision too quickly and that the chosen location was not the most suitable.

As vice-principal it fell to me to go to Ray and share the feelings that had been expressed. It was then that I witnessed a great example of wise leadership. Ray listened to what I told him and decided to postpone the decision for three months, giving time for review and reflection. Three months later, at another meeting with the architect present, all the staff had the opportunity to express their thoughts about the new building and, after discussion, a unanimous decision was reached to build the dining room in a different location. In time, the new dining room was built overlooking the garden and lawns that lay behind the main building. This proved to be a wise and popular decision.

Working with the council

David Morris had brought together on the college council a gifted group of men and women, many of whom had experience of working overseas, and all of whom were in full agreement with the college ethos he had developed. While I was principal, John Dean, who had served for many years with Scripture Union in West Africa, proved to be a great help and support. He would stay one or two nights at the college before and after council meetings, so he could chat with staff and students and get a feel for how things were going. He never interfered with my role as principal but was always a great source of encouragement.

The council left it to the principal, together with the staff, to develop the college and introduce incremental changes as they saw fit. They saw their role as providing fatherly oversight in case some major disaster occurred, or the principal went off the rails! When we were faced with a major decision regarding the finances or the overall programme, they were very willing to help us make the right decision and to ask penetrating questions. On one occasion, there was a real possibility that ANCC might combine with London Bible College (LBC) and form a British equivalent of Fuller Seminary in California, with a theological department and a mission department. I had long discussions with Mike Griffiths, who was then the principal of LBC, and we considered how feasible such a project would be and where it might be located. In the end, with the advice and agreement of the ANCC council, we decided that the ethos of each college was very different and each should continue their development independently.

Developing the curriculum for changing times

One reason we were able to be flexible in adapting the course for each individual student was that the college council and tutorial staff had decided against seeking external accreditation. We wanted the lectures, assignments, and practical courses to be geared to the challenges of cross-cultural ministry rather than the demands of a secular external examination board. A small number of students, who needed an accredited qualification for their future work or to qualify for a visa, were prepared for the Cambridge Diploma of Religious Studies. After some time and discussions with the Open University, it seemed right to develop this course into a BA in Biblical and Cross-cultural Studies.

In 1992, we also launched an accredited Master's Programme. We recognised that those who were going to lead training programmes in their own country needed a higher qualification. This programme was endorsed by the Revd Dick Lucas, the founder of Proclamation Trust, who approved our emphasis on biblical studies. The launch of the programme was attended by the Rt Revd John Taylor, the bishop of St Albans (the diocese in which the college is situated), and the Revd Dr John Stott, who gave the address.

While some students chose to pursue the accredited academic programme, the majority were free during their one or two years in the college to focus on courses relevant to their future ministry. Having studied the history of missionary training both in the West and in the majority world, Rosemary and I have seen many examples where an excellent and relevant training programme was transformed, through the desire for accreditation, into one that became very academic but of less relevance and practical value for the anticipated ministry of the students.

Facing the inevitable problems

Living in close proximity in such a cross-cultural community, it was inevitable that misunderstanding and disagreements would arise. In one year, there were fourteen students from the Netherlands. The Dutch decided the British were dishonest because they never said what they really thought. The British thought the Dutch were rude because they always said exactly what they thought!

A newly arrived Korean female student was shocked when she was greeted with a big hug from a Latin American student whom she had never previously met. She thought he must be a sex maniac, while he thought she was a cold and unfriendly Christian. He wondered if she was a Christian at all! Some Americans were justifiably upset because so many of the bad examples of missionary work quoted by the lecturers were of American missionaries. It was a timely reminder for those who anticipated working in an international mission that, as we had been taught earlier, they might face more unexpected difficulties relating with their fellow missionaries than with local Christians.

The faculty and administrative staff continued to work together harmoniously and were very supportive of me in my leadership role. I was particularly grateful to my Australian PA, Anne Roberts, who provided such efficient support. It was a continual surprise and delight to see the way in which a group of people with such diverse temperaments and gifts could get along so well. There were some strong characters among us, including extroverts who seemingly had to express their opinions just so they could know what they were actually thinking! I sometimes wondered if they were too talkative and just liked the sound of their own voice. That was, until we all took the Myers-Briggs Type Indicator questionnaire, in an attempt to understand more about each other and ourselves. It was then that I realised that staff members who always wanted to go back to square one and examine an issue from every possible angle were not being awkward but being true to their temperament and God-given character. That helped me to be more patient and understanding.

There were times when we received desperately sad news of former students. Within a few weeks of one another, three women who had studied at college died in tragic circumstances: one in a car crash, one in a failed burglary, and one in childbirth. On the opening day of another academic year, we heard that a married couple who had just been studying for a year at the college and who were returning to Nepal for a second three-year missionary term had been killed in an air crash near Kathmandu. Their three young children died with them. Andrew Wilkins, a hydro-engineer, had gone with Interserve to work for a power company in Nepal, advising on dams and hydroelectric projects. His wife, Helen, a social worker, was expecting their fourth child.

It was my responsibility to announce the news to the students gathered for the beginning of the college year. Everyone was deeply shocked, none more so than the other children whose parents were studying at the college. They knew the children who had died and had often played with them. One child asked his mother, "Why didn't Jesus look after them? You told me that Jesus would look after us when we went to Africa."

As the community grieved, we were reminded that Christians are not immune to tragedy or disaster. There is no guarantee of safety just because we are seeking to serve others and share the good news of Jesus with them. Such tragedies force us to retain an eternal perspective on all we do and all that happens to us. We may not understand why God allows such things to happen but we can trust that our lives now and for eternity are in his hands.

Ministry beyond the college

One of the dangers of any residential institution, especially one such as All Nations set in a rural location, is that the staff and students can be cut off from the outside world. In such an ivory tower it is possible to develop all kinds of theories about mission and ministry, which may be totally ineffective and inappropriate in the real world. For this reason, we felt it was important at weekends and vacations for students to be involved in various kinds of church ministry, youth work, and evangelism. Some travelled some distance to places like Luton and inner-city London to be engaged in cross-cultural ministry.

The staff were also engaged in local ministry. In addition, tutors accepted invitations to speak at university Christian Unions and mission conferences, to share some of the lessons we were learning in our multicultural community about the effective communication of the gospel in today's world.

Rosemary and I spoke regularly at Spring Harvest, a large Christian festival held around Easter time. Launched in 1979 as a one-week celebration at Prestatyn in North Wales, it rapidly evolved and within a few years was being held in several locations, and attended by over 50,000 people. We gave seminars at the Minehead site, leading morning sessions with up to a thousand people in a large marquee. It was an immense encouragement to see so many Christians from different denominations, praising God and being eager to learn more about what it means to be a follower of Jesus. One year the theme for Spring Harvest was the work of the Holy Spirit and the organisers prepared a very thorough handbook, setting out in detail the different ways in which Christians understand the work of the Holy Spirit. Despite the diversity of views represented, we were glad that everyone agreed that we are all totally reliant on the work of the Spirit to become more like Christ and more effective in witness. We were disappointed, however, when we led a seminar on cross-cultural mission together with Dr Peter Cotterell, at that time principal of LBC, which was only attended by about thirty people. The previous seminar, held in the same room, had been on the baptism of the Spirit, and had been attended by hundreds! We had supposed that those who wished to be filled with the Spirit might be willing to be sent out by the Spirit!

We continued to be involved in ministry in our local church – Christ Church, Ware. I was invited to preach fairly frequently, though the congregation became rather worried when my sermons were accompanied by "signs and wonders"! Once when I was preaching there was a huge clap of thunder followed by a tropical rainstorm. The church warden's wife had prepared her garden for a barbecue with friends and was not pleased with the outcome of my sermon! On another occasion I was preaching from the first chapter of Isaiah, where the prophet warns God's people of impending judgment. During the sermon I became aware that some of the congregation, seated towards the back of the church, were not listening but appeared rather agitated. I then heard the unmistakable sound of an approaching fire engine. "Has that anything to do with us?" I asked. "Yes," was the reply from the back of the nave. "The church is on fire!" I never understood why the congregation had not said anything when they first noticed smoke rising from the grating in the church floor. They just sat there! Was this a typically English response? I rapidly drew my sermon to a halt and we all quickly evacuated the building. No one was injured. As it turned out, the fire had begun in the boiler room under the church. It was soon put out and the damage was not too extensive.

The following week I returned to the pulpit, this time to preach on Isaiah 6, in which the prophet describes a vision where the Temple is filled with smoke. After my opening prayer, I announced that I, at least, was prepared for any eventuality and showed them the fire extinguisher I had brought with me. Church members never forgot these episodes and, when it was time for us to leave, they composed a song in which they expressed the hope that they would see us again – but not in the pulpit!

During our time at ANCC I was also continuing to be involved in Jewish ministry as the Lausanne associate for Jewish evangelism. This meant setting up international conferences for those concerned to share the gospel with Jewish people. The first of these was held in Newmarket in the UK, where we brought together delegates from seventeen mission agencies. Three years later, we organised another conference at All Nations during the summer vacation. One Canadian visitor was terrified when he found a bat flying around his room. He was afraid to enter the room while his wife sat calmly on a chair in the middle of the room breastfeeding their baby. While he wanted someone to get rid of it, Rosemary told him it was a protected species. Eventually, we managed to throw a sheet over the bat and then release the poor creature into the night.

While we enjoyed working at All Nations, we became increasingly aware of the growing missionary movement in the majority world. We had been challenged and inspired by the many students who came from Africa, Asia, and Latin America. Some had returned home to initiate or develop their own missionary training programmes, and they invited us to visit them.

Sabbatical

In my seventh year as principal, the council graciously allowed us to take a few months' sabbatical. Bob Hunt, as vice-principal, took over my role while we were away. A student had made a life-size cut-out of me and placed it behind my desk in the principal's study. Bob kindly told me that during my absence, no one had noticed any difference!

Rosemary and I decided to spend our sabbatical at Columbia Bible College and Seminary (which later became CIU) in South Carolina. The college was founded in 1923, the same year as All Nations Bible College. Both colleges had a similar doctrinal statement and a commitment to train students to obey the Great Commission. Hundreds of graduates had gone out all over the world to share the gospel, and we were anxious to observe and experience a different model of missionary training.

Although we were not sure at this point how long we should stay at ANCC, we wanted to be available to encourage the development of emerging indigenous training centres around the world. We felt that in addition to the experience we had gained at All Nations, it would be helpful to have some further qualifications in the area of missionary training. The WEAMC was already encouraging networking among training centres around the world and we believed that a period of study at a place like CBCS would serve as good preparation, if we were to become involved in an international ministry.

Rosemary enrolled for the MA in mission. She was excited to read Ruth Tucker's *Guardians of the Great Commission*[1] – about women missionaries of the last two centuries – but observed the women featured were almost all from the Western world. That inspired her to gather the stories of African and Asian women missionaries over the previous few decades. She hoped her findings would encourage more African and Asian women to see how God could use them in cross-cultural mission. She discovered that they were fulfilling all the same roles as their Western counterparts: evangelists and church leaders, medical workers and student workers, Bible teachers and translators, trainers of candidates, and one, Mary Wang, was the head of a large mission based in the UK (Chinese Overseas Christian Mission, COCM). Some came from another major religion and could explain the difference Jesus made in people's lives. When they were working in indigenous missions, they were sometimes pressurised to get married because it was considered normative in the local culture. Many had the advantage of being multilingual. Usually, it was easier for them to adapt to a new culture in their own continent, but a Filipina working in Thailand fitted in so well physically that there was little sympathy for her when first she struggled to speak Thai. Some wives faced difficulties in finding time to learn the required languages, especially if working with an international mission. A Korean wife and mother needed good English to work with Western colleagues, the trade language to communicate in her new country, and a local language for Bible translation. On top of that, she needed to home-school her own children in Korean.

I took the Doctor of Ministry course and, as my thesis, wrote a comparative study on eight missionary training centres in Asia, Africa, and Latin America. I remember the day when I had nearly finished my dissertation, and I discovered to my horror that I had lost the whole thesis! Or so I thought. To my great relief a kind librarian at the college showed me that I had not lost all my work. I had simply left a blank page and that was what I was looking at. The whole manuscript started just one page below!

While we were at the college, we were able to attend an African Methodist Episcopal church. It helped us to understand a little of the culture of the Black community living in the inner city and the encouragement they gave to their children to study hard. We both enjoyed our sabbatical and appreciated the friendship of fellow students and faculty members, especially Dr Kenneth Mulholland and Dr Robert Ferris. We returned to All Nations refreshed and eager for what might lie ahead.

Knowing when to move on

After the people of Israel had camped below Mount Sinai for nearly two years, God said to Moses that they had spent long enough on the mountain and it was time to move on. All Nations is not built on a mountain, but a small hill, but as we drew near to the end of our fourteenth year at the college, we began to wonder if God was telling us that it was time to move. Although we had enjoyed our time there, we began to question whether there was anything further we could bring to the college. Perhaps it was time for us to return to the coalface of mission and to allow someone else to provide vision and leadership for All Nations. We had already begun to visit former students and new mission training programmes in different parts of the world. We were receiving invitations to talk about effective training and to share the mistakes we had made so others could avoid them. As long as I was principal, we did not have the time to accept many invitations. This persuaded us to think more seriously about whether we should leave the college and so be free to encourage the development of indigenous training programmes in other continents. Our feeling that this was the right way forward was confirmed when we heard a lecture given by Dr Bill Taylor when he visited All Nations.[2] He urged the students to go out as servants, willing to do whatever the Lord asked of them. He talked about his admiration for his father, who was willing to give up the comfort and prestige of a leadership position to return to a less prominent ministry of serving others.

When we joined the staff of All Nations, our children were still young. Andrew was eleven and preparing to start secondary school. Ruth was nine, and Catherine only six. Fifteen years later, as we were pondering the way ahead for us, Andrew had already graduated and worked for a computer firm in London, before going to Burkina Faso to do a five-month placement with Wycliffe. He then completed a two-year course at LBC, while at the same time working for Cambridge University Press, before getting married to Jean, whom he had met at his church in London. Ruth had finished her degree and was teaching at a multicultural school in North London. She was learning Russian in preparation to work in St Petersburg for two years with the International Fellowship of Evangelical Students (IFES). Catherine was in the last year of her art degree at the University of Brighton, where she had majored in ceramic sculpture, and had just completed her extended essay on Rembrandt and the Bible. They had all grown up while we were teaching at the college. We were grateful that the Lord had allowed us to remain in the same place through their teenage years. Now they were no longer dependent on us, Rosemary and I thought God might be leading us to further ministry overseas.

We had been appointed as training associates of the WEAMC. At about the same time, Crosslinks, the Anglican mission to which we had been seconded in Ethiopia, was thinking about how it could encourage the missionary movement in the majority world. When they discussed with us the possibility of working with them, it seemed that this was the right way ahead. Our brief would be to travel to different parts of the world to work with those involved in training missionaries in their own country, to assist in the development of new programmes, and to encourage and promote cross-cultural mission and mission training. It was an exciting prospect, but it was going to involve a big upheaval.

Chapter 8
Encouraging
Mission Training Globally

David and Rosemary with Nigerian
missionary trainers, 1994

*For the earth will be filled with the knowledge of
the glory of the Lord as the waters cover the sea.*

Habakkuk 2:14

The ancient Hebrew prophet, Habakkuk, writing 600 years before the birth of Jesus, anticipated a time when people all over the world would come to a personal knowledge of God. In our years at All Nations (1978–93), we saw hundreds of young men and women, gifted by God, going out to every corner of the world to serve others and to bear witness to the good news of Jesus Christ. When we left the college, we were free to travel to many countries in Africa, Asia, and Latin America, where the church was experiencing rapid growth and where Christians had an increasing desire to send out their own missionaries to other parts of the world. They wanted to learn how we had developed our curriculum and what elements of our courses might be relevant in their situation. They were interested to learn from our mistakes as well as from the things that seemed to make the training more effective.

Leaving All Nations brought huge changes. It meant moving from our five-bedroom detached house, set in beautiful woodlands, to a much smaller townhouse in a London suburb. It meant leaving friends and colleagues with whom we had worked for fifteen years and moving to a new area where we knew almost no one. It meant leaving the church where we had worshipped and preached for over twenty years and joining a new congregation of God's people.

It meant leaving a job where our time was largely organised for us around lecturing, pastoring, and administrative duties, and instead beginning a new role for which there was no precedent, no clear structure, and no expectations. It meant leaving work in which we both felt very fulfilled and venturing into something new where it was far from certain how and where we could use the gifts we had developed. For myself, it meant leaving a clearly defined role as college principal where I was supported by a personal assistant and other administrative and technical staff, and moving into a small converted garage space where there was insufficient room for my books and files, and no one to help with my computer which broke down as we left All Nations. It was not an auspicious start. Within two weeks, I felt deflated and discouraged, and began to wonder if we had done the right thing in leaving the college. But a meal out with a former colleague, including a glass of wine, made me feel much better – plus, of course, Rosemary's prayers.

As we began to settle in our new home in Bromley, we sought with the help of both Canon John Ball, head of Crosslinks, and a small support group, to prioritise the numerous invitations we were receiving from different parts of the world. As we responded to those invitations and shared our experiences of training, we learned how Christians in other parts of the world were adapting their programmes to their own context. We then were able to pass on their insights to others as we continued on our travels. Over the next three years, we spoke in fifteen countries and taught at numerous indigenous missionary training programmes, many of which I had written about in my dissertation. In this chapter, we will mainly concentrate on four countries: Korea, Nigeria, India, and Brazil.

Korea

In July 1993 we flew to Korea to teach a group of 180 Korean and Taiwanese students and young professionals, who were interested in mission. These meetings were held in Onnuri Presbyterian Church in Seoul, which had been founded about seven years before by a pastor and twelve families, and which grew to a membership of 75,000. A multimillion-dollar church and administrative complex had been built, and every week more people were coming to faith in Christ. This was the first evidence we saw of the amazing growth of the evangelical church in Korea. We later discovered that some churches were much larger than Onnuri Church, notably Yoiodo Full Gospel Church with its membership of over half a million! At night, the sky above Seoul was illuminated by the hundreds of red crosses on churches shining across the city, illustrating the size of the Christian community. We learned that more police were required to direct the traffic for people going to church on a Sunday than were required to direct traffic for people going to football matches on a Saturday!

The invitation to speak in Korea had come from Ha Yung-In, a former student from All Nations, who was a great prayer warrior. He had developed an amazing ministry among students and young people. Every Thursday evening thousands would gather to worship God and commit themselves to world mission. He launched a training programme for those who felt called to a greater involvement in Christ's mission, and for some years, he kindly invited Rosemary and me to teach these dedicated young people.

Over a period of three weeks, we gave about forty lectures between us on the Bible and mission. We were encouraged by their worship of God, their commitment to Christ and to mission, their eagerness to learn, and the warmth of their hospitality. One moment of embarrassment occurred when I took off my shoes to go into the meeting: those looking after us noticed I had a small hole in my sock. "Sir," they said, "you cannot go into the meeting to teach like that." They rushed across the road to a shopping mall and returned triumphantly with a new pair of socks! In the evening before we were due to leave Korea, Yung-In took me to a tailor's shop and I was measured for a suit. The next day, as we were about to board the plane, the tailor duly appeared with a large parcel, containing the suit and a set of matching shirts and ties. I realised that Korea could become a good place to increase my wardrobe! Rosemary was also given a smart summer suit she was able to wear for weddings and special occasions.

Since hosting the Olympic Games in 1988, the country had been transformed from its traditional isolationist stance to being fully engaged with the rest of the world. It was not only Korean businessmen who wanted to trade across the globe, but also Christian leaders who recognised their opportunity and responsibility to reach out with the gospel. By 1994, South Korean churches had sent out no fewer than 15,000 missionaries. At one annual missionary convention, there were so many people wanting to become missionaries that the organisers were unable to process them all adequately. In consequence it was suggested that they should hold the convention only once every three years. This was to avoid having too many potential missionaries to look after!

Dr David Tai-Woong Lee, who later became the chairman of the WEAMC, had come to All Nations as a visiting lecturer. He had founded GMTC, a leading missionary training centre in Korea, and asked us to come and do some teaching. Over two weeks we taught a group of thirty-five Korean and five Chinese students who were beginning their missionary training. We gave teaching on the theology of mission, communicating to those of other faiths, and bringing up children in another culture. Dr Lee also arranged a three-day seminar for thirty-six Korean missionary trainers from ten different missionary training programmes. He asked me to give nine lectures on such topics as aims and ethos, selection of students and trainers, designing the curriculum, and preparing families. The participants then discussed in Korean how to apply what I said to the Korean context. They were particularly interested in the tutorial system at All Nations, and the pastoral and administrative problems that face missionary trainers.

A lasting memory from our visits to Korea was being present at a missionary rally in the Olympic stadium in Seoul. The focus of the Saturday afternoon rally was to call young Korean men and women to take the gospel of Jesus Christ throughout the world. Despite heavy rain all day, the rally was attended by 60,000 young people who listened eagerly to the speakers and filled the stadium with the sound of their singing. Many answered the appeal to offer themselves for missionary service. We have never been at a missionary meeting like it. It was then that we met Canon James Wong, who invited us to visit Singapore to see if we could help the fast-growing Anglican church there to train prospective missionary candidates.

Nigeria

In November 1993, we flew to Nigeria to attend the Sixth General Assembly of the Association of Evangelicals of Africa and Madagascar (AEAM). We had been told that someone would meet us at Lagos airport, but when we arrived there, no one came to greet us. We waited for an hour or two, before deciding we should take a taxi to a hotel. An elderly Nigerian lady was sitting in the same waiting area next to Rosemary and, though she spoke no English, she realised we were worried. She asked her daughter to find out what was the matter. When they discovered our predicament, they insisted that we did not take a taxi. That would be far too dangerous. They said we should wait for her son who was returning from America, and they would take us to the safety of a hotel. We duly waited and were eventually driven to one nearby, but not before the son had prayed for a safe journey. The next day the daughter returned and kindly drove us to the conference. We discovered that someone had been sent to the airport to meet us but they were looking for a retired college principal. Since I did not look old enough, they assumed I could not be the person they were looking for, and they returned to the conference! Later, we learned that another attendee had taken a taxi from the airport and had been accosted by the driver and some associates demanding a large sum of money. Fortunately, the man was astute enough to say that he had already phoned friends at the conference giving the number of the taxi. That persuaded the taxi driver to take him there without further delay. It made us grateful for God's protection and the kindness of that Nigerian Christian family.

At the conference, we were inspired by meeting and listening to some of the 400 church leaders from all over Africa. It was also amazing not only to see the growth of the Anglican Church but the multiplication of independent evangelical and Pentecostal churches in the city of Lagos. There seemed to be a church on every street corner. Some churches even gathered tens of thousands for services in large warehouses.

In our second week there, the price of petrol rose 700 per cent, strikes and disturbances began, and there was a military coup. We were thankful to leave Lagos and go up to what was then the more peaceful city of Jos in the centre of the country. There we stayed with Bayo and Naomi Famanure, who had founded

Calvary Ministries (CAPRO) and Agape Missions. They had also established a missionary training centre for Nigerian graduates. They initially set up a course lasting four months, but the students complained it was too condensed and they could not possibly take in everything they were being taught. So, the course was extended, first to six months and then to nine. No one paid any fees. They made their own bricks to put up their own buildings, grew vegetables, and prayed that God would supply whatever money they needed. A strong emphasis was laid on developing the character of these graduates and in their final assessment, more marks were given for their relational skills and their effectiveness as evangelists than for their written work. After nine months of training, the students were sent to a village, unreached with the gospel, to share the good news of Jesus.

On one occasion, Bayo took us to a remote village to see how the students were getting on with their ministry placement. Prior to their arrival, the village chief had erected a large hut which, he said, could either be a mosque for Muslims if they came first, or a church if Christians came first. By the time we got to the village, the students had already been there for three months. They had started a small school and virtually all the villagers wanted to be baptised. The chief was happy for that, though he said he would not be baptised himself, as he did not want to upset their local spirit god.

When we left Jos, we travelled to Ibadan to visit Revd Canon Isaac Ogungbile, a former All Nations student, and Bishop Gideon Olajide. Rosemary preached in the cathedral at the annual service of the Mothers' Union, a women's movement of the Anglican Church, which seeks to support families worldwide. I spoke at the graduation of the first eighty-four lay evangelists for the diocese and the dedication of a new Anglican church. The church had been given the name "Jesus Christ's Ambassadors' Evangelical Anglican Church". It had started eleven months before when a small group of believers began to meet in a wooden hut in a poorer part of the city. That was in January. Now it was December and the few believers had become a congregation of nearly a thousand. They had already planted a "baby" church in one adjacent district and started a house-group in another. The bishop modestly commented: "We have planted fifteen churches in this city in the last four years, and each of them has over 500 members today." We felt the Anglican Church in Nigeria could teach the church in the UK much about church growth!

Nigeria had become a major missionary-sending country in the developing world. By 2010, there were numerous Nigerian mission agencies supporting 9,000 missionaries serving in 57 countries. The particular burden of Nigerian Christians is to take the gospel to the many unreached peoples within their own country, but they are also aware of their responsibility towards other countries in North and West Africa, and the Middle East, where they can travel with fewer restrictions than is the case for Westerners and at less cost.

While the indigenous missionary movement had begun in Nigeria in the 1940s with the founding of the Evangelical Missionary Society, the situation was rather different in Kenya. Although the church in Kenya was growing steadily, only in the last few years had a mission agency been founded. The Africa Inland Church had started their own mission, but many congregations did not see cross-cultural mission as their responsibility. Students we met at the Africa Inland Missionary Training Centre in Eldoret shared with us that when they felt called to be missionaries they were told, "If you want to be a missionary, go to the foreign missionaries for support." Even if we were discouraged by this attitude, we were encouraged by the centre. It was not a theological college. It was assumed that students would have completed theological, biblical, and pastoral studies before they came to Eldoret for their missionary training. The college was not seeking to provide academically accredited theological study, but rather vocational training for missionaries.

The course aimed to prepare students academically, practically, and spiritually for their future ministry. Not only were the students trained in cross-cultural evangelism and church-planting, but they were also given a wide variety of basic practical skills so that they would be able to cope with life in a different culture or a remote environment. The programme offered family-based missionary training. The steering committee had decided at the outset that each candidate should bring his wife and children with him. The housing provided was designed for families and a nursery school had been set up so that husbands and wives could both attend classes. Some additional teaching was provided for the wives who only had minimal formal education.

India

After P. S. Thomas had spent a term at All Nations as a visiting lecturer, he invited us to visit India and teach at the Outreach Training Institute (OTI), run by the Indian Evangelical Mission (IEM). IEM, founded in the 1960s, was one of a growing number of Indian agencies sending their own missionaries cross-culturally within India and to many countries beyond. When we attended the annual conference of the Indian Missions Association (IMA) in 1994, we learned that there were 10,000 Indian missionaries, making it one of the largest mission-sending countries in the world. Ten years later, when we met the head of the IMA in Singapore, he told us there were at least 30,000 missionaries sent out by Indian churches, but they had stopped counting. Most of these were involved in cross-cultural work, reaching out to the under-privileged and marginalised people groups in India, and also to the Hindu heartlands.

Rosemary, who enjoyed teaching on the history of Christian mission, was pleased to visit the Indian Missionary Society, based in Tirunelveli. It had been founded in 1903 by Bishop Samuel Azariah, the first Indian Anglican bishop. Towards the end of the twentieth century, the society was supporting more than a thousand Indian missionaries sharing the gospel and planting churches in the north of India and throughout South Asia. While in India we also visited Vellore Hospital, founded initially for women by an American missionary, Dr Ida Scudder, in 1900, and nearly a century later it was still providing exceptional medical care for the whole country.

P. S. Thomas was convinced that missionaries serving with IEM must be trained properly. He was aware of the problems, and in some cases, the tragedies, that could result when missionaries were sent out with little or no preparation, and he regularly shared his own experience as an example.

Some years before, he had set out from South India with a close friend who, like him, was highly committed to the Lord and felt called to be a missionary. They had had four years of theological training at Union Biblical Seminary, one of the best colleges in India. They were aware of the enormous spiritual needs in northern India and wanted to go to the most difficult area to plant churches. They had prayed individually and together for North India throughout the four years in seminary.

Two months after graduation, the two friends travelled to a remote Himalayan valley, sent by one of the most reputable indigenous missions in India. They did not know the proper route to the place of their calling; they eventually reached their destination, but by a much longer way than was necessary! In addition, the two did not know the climatic conditions there. Although it was the height of the North India summer, they found to their horror that they could not sleep without heating in the room. They had arrived with very little warm clothing and did not know how to live in such a cold place. They had not been adequately prepared for life in a totally different culture or for the spiritual battle that they encountered. Faced with the challenge of learning the local language, they developed their own method of language learning, which turned out to not be very successful! After many years, they were still speaking the host language with a heavy South Indian accent, and they seemed to be making little progress in bringing these people to faith in Christ. In fact, within six months, one of them was questioning whether Jesus was God incarnate or a man made into a god by his followers.

In addition, the missionaries did not know how to handle loneliness. When P. S. Thomas married before they left, he had assumed that if his wife was committed to the Lord and willing to be the wife of a poor missionary, that would be enough. He married without much preparation for marriage or any advice on raising a family in such a context. When children arrived, too quickly and too frequently, neither of the parents knew how to take care of them in a cold climate and a different culture. During their long first term the wife's emotional health deteriorated. They began to suspect each other's commitment and spirituality. They did not know how and where to educate their children. They thought it was unspiritual to talk about their own problems to others, particularly to their mission leaders.

The two friends had undergone four years of seminary training before they went to North India, but this hadn't prepared them for cross-cultural life and witness. They had come with a vision to plant churches in one of the most difficult places, but after five years, one of them left North India with a sense of failure and guilt. The other became convinced of the need for cross-cultural missionary training and set up IEM's training centre. He knew that commitment to the Lord and a high motivation for missions are essential, but this was not enough to produce an effective cross-cultural missionary.

Brazil

Over the past 100 years, the evangelical churches in Latin America have experienced rapid growth. New evangelical churches have been planted almost on a daily basis. On one occasion, I preached at a church that had started eleven months earlier as the result of a telephone counselling ministry; it already had fifty members. One Brazilian who had studied at All Nations bought a large tent and started a new church in São Paulo. Within a few months, over a hundred people were attending every week.

As the number of evangelical Christians in Brazil grew, many believed the time had come to assume their responsibility for taking the gospel into all the world. They felt they must now continue the work of world evangelisation, which for so long had been in the hands of Western Christians. Some pastors used the metaphor of a relay race in which the baton of world evangelisation was being handed from the West to the countries of the majority world.

This growing sense of commitment to global evangelisation was not limited to Brazil but was seen throughout the subcontinent.

In 1987, I was invited to attend the first Ibero-American mission conference, COMIBAM, held in São Paulo, Brazil. Over 4,000 Christians from every country in Latin America took part and the conference was conducted in Spanish – with translations into Portuguese and English (fortunately). Speaker after speaker shared their vision for world mission and their desire to see Latin Americans going into the whole world with the gospel. Within a few years, thousands of missionaries from the continent had set out to take the good news across Latin America and to other parts of the world.

In 1995, Rosemary and I were able to go to Brazil and Argentina together and to visit Bible colleges and training centres. One of the first missionary training centres to be established in Brazil ("The Valley of Blessing") had been set up by a Brazilian mission called Missao Antioquia (Antioch Mission). The training programme lasted for eleven months with the intention to prepare candidates for service in Latin America, Portuguese-speaking Africa, Europe, and parts of Asia. An essential part of the training they received was to spend six months in Bolivia gaining experience in cross-cultural life and work. This time provided a test for developing ministry skills and an opportunity to enhance cultural sensitivity. The Antioch Mission placed strong emphasis on the spiritual preparation of its candidates. In one part of the land owned by the training centre was a small valley set aside for prayer. A sign reminded people that this valley was intended to be used "for praying, not kissing"! In the centre of the valley was a chapel, called the House of Prayer, with a larger room for group prayer and several cubicles for individual prayer.

The training included courses on spiritual warfare, exorcism, and how to minister to those who had been involved in spiritism. Many Brazilians believe in the existence of evil spirits and, in many cases, they have lived their lives in a state of fear. Those who taught in the Valley of Blessing had been engaged in exorcism.

They were familiar with the realities of spiritual warfare and were well equipped to prepare their students to minister in this area.

While in Latin America, Rosemary and I were also able to visit the Cordoba Bible Institute in Argentina, which offered specialist courses on mission. Dr Jonathan Lewis, who was born in Argentina of missionary parents, taught on the faculty and was deeply involved in promoting missions and the training of missionaries in Argentina and throughout Latin America. When he took missionary candidates on practical mission experience, he insisted that they took only the bare minimum of equipment because they were going to live among people who had very few possessions. This meant they were not allowed to take any shampoo or even toothpaste!

International Missionary Training Fellowship

After we left All Nations, we had been working as mission partners of Crosslinks and training consultants with the Mission Commission of the World Evangelical Alliance. The aim of the Mission Commission was to promote dynamic cooperation among existing and emerging national and regional mission associations, and to aid the development of training programmes and support structures. In 1986, Dr Bill Taylor had been appointed as its director. Under his leadership, the IMTF was established as the first global network of cross-cultural missionary trainers and centres. A number of key books were published on the critical topic of missionary training, including a *World Directory of Missionary Training Programmes*, edited by Dr Ray Windsor, the former principal of ANCC. The book included the details of more than 500 mission training centres around the world.[1] Dr Jonathan Lewis, who welcomed us to Cordoba, played a large part in promoting inter-agency cooperation in mission and mission training, serving as a training consultant and director of publications.

As we visited centres in these three continents from 1993 to 1996, we were continually impressed by the way in which they adapted their training and teaching methodology according to their cultural context. Their programmes included a wide variety of components adapted to the local culture and the intended ministry of the students, such as: coping with culture shock; training husbands and wives together; preparing the children; developing communication skills (including cross-cultural communication); learning how to use modern technology; gaining practical skills relevant to the context (for example, raising goats, maintaining motorbikes, making simple solar ovens, or coping where there is no doctor!).

Their primary concern was not to provide an academic qualification, but to develop curricula based on the needs of the individual trainee and the observed needs of the people among whom they would serve. They gave great importance to training that was practical, relevant, and holistic, as these two examples from Nigeria and India demonstrate.

> *Our purpose is to provide practical training in cross-cultural ministry skills to people called of God and committed to cross-cultural missionary work. Our training is not geared towards giving paper qualifications to students, but towards making them effective field missionaries.[2]*

> *The Outreach Training Institute is not a regular Theological Seminary or a Bible School. The training imparted is an integration of academic excellence, spiritual growth and practical ministry. The emphasis of the training is to prepare people for cross-cultural ministry.[3]*

While these centres continue to adapt their training programmes to the changing times and new challenges faced by their students, other new centres are being developed all over the world. The content, duration, and medium of the training they offer vary according to the context and the nature of the anticipated ministries. What is critical in any programme for training missionaries is that the preparation is not reduced to a bare minimum or even neglected altogether. As we travelled around the world, we observed that some churches and mission agencies provided only minimal preparation to their candidates or, in some cases, no training at all. Those they sent out struggled to cope with the challenges and demands of cross-cultural ministry, never learning how to live in and adapt to a different culture. They and their families could not settle in their new context and often returned home sooner than they anticipated. In 1987, the WEAMC published the results of extensive research, which identified inadequate pre-field training as one of the primary causes for missionary attrition.[4]

Although we witnessed some examples, both in the West and in other parts of the world, where candidates were inadequately prepared, we were constantly impressed and inspired by the rapid growth of the missionary movement in Asia, Africa, and Latin America, and encouraged by the emergence of numerous excellent programmes that were being developed to train indigenous missionaries. It was a joy to see those who had been receiving missionaries for so many years, now sending out their own missionaries, and to visit parts of the world like Latin America, which had been a mission "field", but which now had become a mission force.

Chapter 9
Singapore and World Mission

Bishop Rennis Ponniah, vicar at
St John's—St Margaret's, Singapore
when we joined in 1996

*"You are worthy to take the scroll and to open
its seals, because you were slain, and with your
blood you purchased for God persons from every
tribe and language and people and nation. You
have made them to be a kingdom and priests to
serve our God, and they will reign on the earth."*

Revelation 5:9–10

Asians with a passion for mission

Where should we go next? In the summer of 1995, we had visited Singapore and spent two very enjoyable months there teaching at the Discipleship Training Centre (DTC). The centre had been established by David Adeney, an English missionary who had served for many years in China and East Asia with the China Inland Mission, InterVarsity Fellowship, and the International Fellowship of Evangelical Students. He founded DTC in 1968 with the intention of providing biblical and ministerial training for Asian graduates.

Our two months at DTC reminded us how much we enjoyed teaching and interacting with a multicultural group of highly motivated mature students... who spoke English! When we were invited to return to DTC to teach and for me to assume the role of dean, it seemed right to accept for a number of reasons. First, Singapore had become a global travel hub and would be an ideal location from which we could continue to serve as training consultants in the Two-Thirds or Majority World. Secondly, we knew that Christians in Singapore had a growing desire to be involved in international mission and wanted to emulate the example of the church in Antioch that sent out missionaries like Paul and Barnabas (Acts 13).

Some were surprised at our decision to move to Singapore. Our vicar in England asked why, having been principal of a college of nearly 200, I felt it right to lead a community of twelve to fifteen. Rosemary commented, rather cheekily, that Jesus was content to spend three years training a dozen disciples, so perhaps that was not a bad model.

We moved to Singapore in June 1996 and felt at home very quickly. Singapore enjoys one of the highest standards of living in the world, is efficiently run, and immaculately clean. Those who drop litter are liable to a fine, which is reflected on the popular T-shirts that carry the slogan: "Singapore is a fine city." The temperature is consistently about 32 degrees Celcius, which means it is always hot and humid. We thoroughly enjoyed the cleanliness, the efficient public transport system, the variety of food, and even the climate, knowing we could always escape from the heat into air-conditioned rooms. DTC is set in the middle of a small garden at the end of a quiet cul-de-sac not far from the city centre. The main building has a large lounge/dining room, library, lecture room, offices for the staff, and accommodation for the students. In a separate building there are three apartments for staff.

The students at DTC, mainly university graduates, came from all over South and East Asia, including Pakistan, India, Thailand, South Korea, Japan, Indonesia, Malaysia, and Singapore. The two-year course did not offer an accredited degree. Those who came did so because they wanted a period of training for ministry that combined biblical and cultural studies, a strong focus on spiritual life, and the opportunity to live in and learn from a multicultural community. The students spent some time each week in ministry outside the college and it was encouraging to hear stories of people coming to Christ through their witness. A student who witnessed among construction workers from mainland China brought two of them to faith. Another worked in a drug rehabilitation centre and led one of the girls to Christ.

After they had finished their training, many students went back to their own country to engage in student ministry or Bible teaching. Others joined mission agencies to be evangelists or Bible translators. One returned to Pakistan, where he served for over twenty years as the general secretary of the Pakistan Fellowship of Evangelical Students. A student from Thailand returned to teach in a Bible school in Bangkok. An Indian went from Tamil Nadu in the south of India to the north to work as a missionary. Inspired by seeing the gravestone of an English missionary to India in his home town, he reflected, "If this English missionary was willing to come so far to share the good news of Jesus with the people of India, shouldn't I also be willing to do the same for my own people?"

There was a very small staff at DTC and we particularly enjoyed working with a Chinese Singaporean couple, Kua Wee Seng and

Cheng. Cheng provided excellent pastoral care for the students and often overstretched herself by giving them so much of her time. Wee Seng had a strong desire to see Singaporeans serving as "tentmaker" missionaries, using their professional skills as an opportunity to live and work in countries that were otherwise closed to Christian witness. Together, we designed an evening course, called TENT. We expected only twelve to attend the introductory residential weekend for potential "tentmakers"; in the end, thirty came. Three of them had to sleep in a classroom because all the bedrooms were full.

The small size of the community at DTC meant it was still possible for us to be involved in ministry farther afield in Asia and beyond. On one occasion we were invited to spend two days with the faculty of the Theological Seminary of Malaysia (TSM) to talk about the tutorial system and the training philosophy developed at All Nations. While I was there, I received an invitation to consider heading up a seminary in the USA, but that did not seem to fit our calling to help forward missionary training in the Two-Thirds World. I asked the principal of TSM, Dr Hwa Yung, who later became the Methodist bishop of West Malaysia, for his advice on whether Rosemary and I should go to the USA or stay in Asia. He encouraged us to stay and said how much he appreciated having people who could share their insights and experience but were willing to serve in partnership with the local church and under national leadership.

We had offered to work in DTC for two or three years while the board looked for an Asian dean. In our second year, we asked a visiting Japanese pastor, who had studied at the centre, how long we should stay at DTC. "As long as you stay there," he said, "the board will have no incentive to look for your replacement." That seemed to make sense and was a salutary reminder that missionaries can sometimes hinder the natural development of churches or institutions by staying too long.

Our earlier concern for the Jewish people remained and we still ministered to Jewish Christians in various ways, but we also

135

recognised that Jesus told the disciples that their mission was to the world and not just to the Jewish nation. For some time, Trinity Theological College (TTC) in Singapore had been seeking to develop a mission track in their Master of Divinity programme and Dr John Chew, who was at that time principal of the college, invited us to join the staff. The following two years we taught at Trinity, a college that had been established for the training of Anglican, Presbyterian, Methodist, and Lutheran pastors. I taught courses on the theology and practice of mission, with input from Rosemary on the history of Christian mission. She also taught a course on the missionary message of Acts, which proved to be very popular. Once again, we enjoyed being part of a vibrant community of Asian Christians, as we helped them to prepare for ministry. One challenge that I faced at the beginning of a course on preaching was the reluctance of some students in the class to give expository sermons or preach on doctrine. "Doctrine is boring," they said. "We want to give sermons that are full of miraculous and exciting stories." To which I replied, "We believe in a God who has created such an incredibly beautiful world, and a Saviour who gave up everything because he loved us, and the Spirit who transforms our hearts and lives! If that is boring, the problem does not lie with the doctrine but with the preacher!"

During our time at TTC, Dr Hwa Yung, the principal of TSM in Malaysia, was appointed as the first director of the new Centre for the Study of Christianity in Asia (CSCA) at TTC in Singapore and, though he was unable to be in college for a year, he invited me to assist him in the setting up of this new research centre and to serve as his assistant director. I was convinced of the significance of this centre as the churches of Asia were becoming increasingly engaged in the task of mission throughout the region, and I was delighted to serve in this interim position.

Anglicans with a vision for growth

When we arrived in Singapore in 1996, we asked the Anglican bishop, Dr Moses Tay, which church we should attend.

He suggested St John's–St Margaret's (SJSM) as a church which had well-led worship, good expository preaching, an active student ministry, and a keen desire to be involved in cross-cultural ministry in East Asia. When we went to the church, the vicar, the Revd Rennis Ponniah, commented with a smile that perhaps we had been sent to check up on him. He welcomed us with open arms, and while we were there, Rosemary and I were both invited to preach, as well as to teach evening courses on biblical books.

It was so encouraging to worship in an Anglican church that had nearly a thousand members and began each service with thirty to forty minutes of worship, led by talented musicians and a gifted worship leader who always prepared thoroughly.

The majority of church members belonged to a cell (or home) group. When someone had professed faith in Christ, they were asked to complete a new believers' course before being invited to join a cell group. Those who were responsible for the organising of cell groups were not quite sure what to do with us, although I think they believed we were Christians. Eventually, we were invited to join a cell that was led by a very able couple, Andy Lim and Hwee Hua, who had highly successful careers in business and financial services. Hwee Hua also served for many years as a Member of Parliament in Singapore and, in 2009, she was the first woman to be appointed to the Cabinet.

A typical cell group meeting began around eight o'clock with a time of singing followed by the sharing of news and requests for prayer. Then we studied a biblical passage before having a time of prayer. At about ten o'clock we would start having food, a favourite Singaporean activity. It is said that Singaporeans have only one meal a day. It starts in the morning and continues till late at night. We were often amused that even after we had been in the country for ten years, those who did not know us would ask us if we ate Chinese food.

It became a highlight of our week to attend the cell group, spend time with our Singaporean friends, and grow with them in our commitment to Christ. One man, called Thian Chye, whose wife,

Gem, attended the cell, had never shown much interest in the gospel, but when he was diagnosed with bowel cancer, Gem said it was a good time for him to start thinking about Jesus. He came to faith and, subsequently, to the astonishment of his surgeons, survived numerous operations. His testimony brought several others to faith, including Catherine, who was suffering from mouth cancer. When Catherine first attended our cell group meetings, she expressed how bitter she felt that God had allowed this to happen to her. However, when Thian Chye shared that after he believed in Jesus, God took away his fear of his next operation and his possible death, Catherine also came to believe.

Alan enjoyed playing golf with his wife, Angela, on Sundays, while their children were attending children's church. After Angela became a Christian, Alan surprised her the first time he came to the cell group, by sharing some of the problems he had faced as a young man. After he came to personal faith in Jesus, he and his wife not only led a cell group but also ran Bible studies for construction workers from mainland China who worked in Singapore. They saw many come to faith.

Stephen was a very successful lawyer, who had little interest in Christianity. Over time, his wife and his three children professed faith in Christ. They all wanted to be baptised, but as the day for their baptism drew near, Stephen learned that their eldest son was not going to be baptised. He asked him why he had changed his mind. "I am waiting for you, Dad," was the reply. Stephen was so moved that he also came to accept Christ, so the whole family could rejoice together in their new-found faith.

One year, Pastor Rennis, who later became the bishop of Singapore, challenged each cell group to bring at least three people to Christ over the next twelve months. The members of our cell group found it hard to believe that within a year we could lead three new people to faith in Christ. Imagine our delight and surprise when the following December fourteen people were baptised as the result of the witness of the members of our cell. In a short time, the church grew to nearly 2,000 members. Even so, it was not the biggest

Anglican church in Singapore. One had over 5,000 members and the cathedral was larger, running thirteen different services in different languages and styles of worship each weekend.

Since Rosemary was given only one course to teach at TTC, she accepted an invitation from Pastor Rennis to become the honorary mission pastor at SJSM, responsible under him for the selection, training, and pastoral oversight of the church's long-term missionaries. She loved working as a member of the staff team at the church and found many wishing to discuss missionary service. She was helped by Chua Kim Yien, who had served for two years as the assistant to the previous mission pastor. Over the next few years, several members of the church trained and went out as mission partners to other countries in East Asia. Kim Yien served for eleven years as a missionary in Northeast Thailand before returning to Singapore to serve on the staff team of the church. After Kim Yien left for Thailand, Rosemary was assisted by another lady before she served in China for many years.

One difficult issue faced by new Christians was the reaction of their parents. Chinese parents expect that, after their death, their children will faithfully perform the appropriate rituals at their funeral and so facilitate their passage to the afterlife. It was inherent in Chinese culture that one should continue to respect and honour one's parents in both this life and the next. Many of those who came to faith in Jesus felt they could not continue to offer prayers and sacrifices for their deceased parents, though they would continue to honour their memory. Will was the eldest and favourite son of his father, but when he became a Christian, his father was furious and virtually disowned him.

There was so much to admire in these Singaporean Christians, quite apart from their willingness to face the disapproval and criticism of their families. Because they had not previously belonged to a church, virtually all their friends were non-Christians and they were happy to share their new-found faith with them. They were less inhibited than those of us in Britain seem to be. They would find it quite natural to pray in the street or in a restaurant.

We remember attending a dinner after a baptism and chatting with a group of the candidate's non-Christian friends. After a short while, Stephen's wife, Karen, joined our group and within thirty seconds, she was talking about Jesus in a very natural and inoffensive way.

A church member, Lee Choy Ping, who had worked as an editor in Singapore, encouraged me to write a book on Abraham. She proved to be an excellent editor, often correcting my grammar and spelling. "How can you do that?" I asked her. "You're Chinese and I'm English!" She just smiled. When the book was eventually published as *By Faith and Failure*,[1] 600 copies were sold at SJSM in the first weekend. The book was subsequently translated into several Asian languages. Ping then encouraged me to write another book on Exodus, which was entitled *By Word and Wonders*.[2] She is currently editing our third book in this series on Leviticus, Numbers, and Deuteronomy, under the title *By Law and Love*. Ping and her husband, Paul, have remained among our closest friends.

Partners in global mission

During the five years we were teaching at DTC and TTC, we continued to travel and speak about mission. In one year, we visited nine different Asian countries, including Sri Lanka, where we were invited to speak on mission in the Anglican cathedral in Colombo. When we arrived at the airport, we were greeted with the news that we were to give twenty-four lectures on mission in the next few days. We felt a surge of panic as most of our notes on mission were in Singapore. Thankfully, God helped us to remember sufficient salient points and we managed to cope adequately. Fortunately, our Sri Lankan host interceded on our behalf and demanded that the number of lectures be reduced.

Other memorable visits included leading a retreat for the Anglican clergy of the Colombo and Kandy dioceses, giving Bible talks at a conference of 400 students in New Delhi, speaking on John's Gospel at a house party of 200 Singaporean students in Malaysia, and addressing a large conference on mission organised by Episcopalians in the USA.

In the Malaysian capital of Kuala Lumpur, I was invited to participate in a conference that considered the question, "Do we still need missionary societies?" A Malaysian pastor who addressed this question came from a church that had over 5,000 members. It was a vibrant, rapidly growing church, reaching out in the suburbs of Kuala Lumpur. It had already sent out several missionaries. The pastor said, "We have the resources, we have the personnel, we have the vision. There should be no reason why we cannot send out missionaries by ourselves without any need to depend on the foreign missions who have worked here in Malaysia for so long." He paused, and then continued: "But the truth is we do not have the experience or the expertise of these long-established mission agencies." He then went on to express his conviction that they needed to work alongside these agencies and to learn from them, if they were to succeed in their missionary endeavour and avoid unnecessary mistakes.

The pastor told the story of a young couple who had been sent out from their church a few years earlier. The couple had responded to the call to missionary service at the culmination of a week's teaching on mission. Within a few weeks they were sent out to another Asian country. They were given words of encouragement but no formal training or preparation. They struggled for two years but discovered they were unable to cope with the pressures and challenges of life there. Depressed and ashamed, they returned home to Malaysia to apologise to their church for their failure. As he recounted this sad story, the pastor commented that it was not the couple who had failed, but the church that sent them.

I was asked to respond and agreed with him that mission agencies can play a role in assisting the national church, but I said I knew some foreign missions were reluctant to work with, or under, the leadership of national churches. I acknowledged that missionaries who were sent out from the West were only part of the international family of witnesses, and they should no longer be the ones who always led a team or determined strategy. They needed to work alongside others and increasingly under national leadership.

During our early years in Singapore, we both tried to continue our own studies. Rosemary had previously completed a master's degree from Columbia International University (formerly CBCS), majoring on the contribution of African and Asian women in mission. While we were spending a sabbatical at the Overseas Ministries Study Center (OMSC) in the USA, she studied for a Master of Theology in Missiology, focusing on the role of women in mission, from the University of South Africa. She didn't realise it would begin with a study of Western feminist theology, but was able to focus on the lives of African-American and Asian women theologians.

Her final research focused on the role of women in the church in Myanmar. She made several visits to Myanmar and read assignments on the issue that students at the Myanmar Institute of Theology had written for their degrees. She showed how their rereading of the Bible through the eyes of women, and their research into the traditions of their own people groups, had led many of these graduates to challenge the commonly accepted cultural and religious norms of their own people that are negative towards women. They envisaged a church that was truly a partnership of equals, women and men sharing in ministry, decision-making and leadership, and together seeking to open the kingdom of God to all the peoples of Myanmar, including especially the despised and the marginalised.

As Rosemary worked on her thesis, I was researching the history of the training of missionaries in the UK during the twentieth century. I wanted to concentrate on the development of All Nations and its distinctive pattern of holistic training. We had met Dr Jan Jongeneel, Professor of Missiology at the University of Utrecht in the Netherlands, while we were at OMSC. When he learned of my research, he encouraged me to pursue my studies and submit them as a doctoral thesis. He offered to be my supervisor, and we agreed on the basic structure and focus of the research. As my writing progressed, I would send a finished chapter off to him in the Netherlands and would invariably receive it back within two weeks covered in a number of corrections, alterations, and suggestions.

On one occasion, after sending off a mammoth chapter, I heard nothing back for several months. I began to wonder what had happened to Dr Jongeneel. I rang up with some fear and trepidation and was greatly relieved when his wife answered the phone and said he was just finishing his breakfast. It transpired that my chapter had arrived safely and he had spent many hours going over it before posting it back. Somewhere between the Netherlands and Singapore, the chapter had been lost. "That's no problem," said Dr Jongeneel. "Just send it to me again and I will go over it once more."

True to his word, that was exactly what he did, going over the manuscript a second time and then sending it back within a few days. I feel greatly indebted to such a dedicated supervisor who was so thorough in the way he went through his students' work and was so committed to helping them in every possible way. It set a high standard for me to follow when I was asked to supervise the work of doctoral students.

Time off

We were always advised to take time out from a busy ministry to relax. Singapore, despite being a small city state, has preserved many green spaces especially around reservoirs. We enjoyed going for walks, but our favourite places were Sungei Buloh, a nature reserve, which lay in the north of Singapore, and Pulau Ubin, a small island fifteen minutes' boat ride away. Both offered the opportunity of getting away from the noise and bustle of the city to see monitor lizards, monkeys, otters, wild boar, the occasional crocodile, plus a huge variety of birds. More than 400 species of birds have been recorded in Singapore, among them eight different kinds of brightly coloured kingfishers. I soon invested in a good pair of binoculars and gave Rosemary a pair as a birthday gift, since it wasn't too interesting for her to keep hanging about while I looked for a tiny bird on top of a tree. We spent many enjoyable hours admiring the variety of bird calls, the brightness of their plumage, and the patterns of their behaviour. We praised God for the beauty of his creation and were particularly excited when we saw a new (to us) species for the first time.

When we were invited to speak in other Asian countries, we tried, if possible, to add a couple of days at the end of our schedule to relax by visiting some good birding locations. When we took our holidays, we often chose places that had a good reputation for their birdlife. I usually bought a book about the birds in each country we visited and soon built up a large collection of books on the birds of Asia. We were even able to enthuse other members of the mission to start birdwatching as a hobby and means of relaxation. I remember the first time we persuaded David and Ruth Gould, colleagues at OMF international centre in Singapore, to visit Pulau Ubin with us. We saw a number of fascinating birds and heard the distinctive call of a woodpecker. Without hesitation and with no thought for his safety, David dived into the jungle and disappeared as he searched for the bird. He has proved in time to be even more enthusiastic and knowledgeable about birds than we are!

Meanwhile, back in the UK...

Inevitably, we missed our family back home, even though we were able to return to the UK for a month once a year. Our first grandson, Noah, was born to Andrew and Jean in 1995, when we were teaching in Singapore. Then our second grandson was born two years later, and again we were miles away in Singapore. He was duly registered as Samuel Andrew Solomon, but he was so angelic his mother preferred to call him Gabriel, which is the name by which he has subsequently been known.

One evening, in November 1997, I had a phone call from a handsome Irish dentist named Colin Flanagan who had met our daughter Ruth while they were both studying at All Nations. He asked if he could marry our daughter. On a very hot day in August 1998 they were married in Christ Church, Ware, and their reception was held at All Nations. The following year, our younger daughter, Catherine, also married.

Chapter 10
General Director of
OMF International

OMF International Council, 2003

*"Forget the former things; do not dwell on
the past. See, I am doing a new thing!"*

Isaiah 43:18–19a

Unexpected invitation

Although we enjoyed our time at TTC, we soon began to realise that there was not a full-time job for either of us there. After the principal had invited us to teach courses on the history, theology, and practice of missions, we discovered another couple had also been appointed to teach similar subjects. The college was planning to launch a mission track for their Master of Divinity degree and wanted to make sure they had sufficient faculty. At the same time, some of the staff were making the very reasonable suggestion that, in an Asian college, it would be appropriate to have Asians teaching courses on mission. As mentioned previously, Rosemary only taught one course on the missionary message of Acts and, although it proved extremely popular, she was not asked to do any more. I had some mission courses but was also asked to teach homiletics. I discussed the situation with the new principal, Dr Robert Solomon, with whom we had a very good relationship. He explained that, while on a personal level he loved having us at the college, there was not enough work for us to do.

This left us in something of a quandary. Should we return to the UK? Should we consider working in Africa, or Asia, or another part of the world? A number of options were open to us but, as we prayed about them, it did not seem right to move away from Asia or even from Singapore. In August 2000, we wrote in a prayer letter that we were praying about the future. Soon afterwards, we received a phone call from David Pickard, the general director of OMF International, inviting us to lunch. We enjoyed a pleasant meal with him and his wife, Sue, talking about one thing and another, until Sue kicked her husband under the table and muttered, "Get on with it!" At which point David asked whether we would allow my name to go forward for consideration as his possible successor.

This was a total surprise. We had much respect for the mission, which had been founded by Hudson Taylor as the China Inland Mission in 1865. It was one of the largest and most respected international mission agencies. We knew the mission was looking for a new general director but never considered that I was the right person for the job at this stage in our career. Rosemary, in particular, had been praying that OMF would find the right person, but never thought that we might be the answer to her prayers.

As we overcame our surprise, I explained to David Pickard that, as I was approaching sixty, I thought I was too old for the position and, in any case, I had left the job of principal at All Nations in part to leave behind the responsibility and burden of leadership. I was aware that I could cope with organisation and administration, but did not feel that was my primary gifting. David responded to my concerns by saying that although there had previously been an age limit of sixty for those in senior leadership roles in OMF, it had been agreed to lay that rule aside in the case of the general director. He also said they were not looking for an administrator, but for someone who was pastoral, gifted in Bible teaching, and who could help the mission reflect theologically on its role in Asia. After listening to his comments and subsequently reflecting on our conversation, we began to wonder if this might be what God was calling us to do.

When we made a short visit to the UK, we were able to discuss this possibility with members of the mission committee of Christ Church, Bromley, our main supporting church in the UK. The committee consisted of very wise and well-informed people with a lot of experience in overseas mission. As we talked and prayed with them about this new direction in our lives, it seemed right to them and to us to allow our names to go forward.

Rosemary and I were asked to submit written statements about our experience and understanding of mission. The next step in October 2000 was a formal interview, which lasted a whole day. The interviewing panel, consisting of twelve mission personnel and board members, had read through our papers and they grilled us with numerous questions. One person asked me what I thought about leading the large ship of OMF. To which I replied, "I think it will be a bit like steering the Titanic and I hope it does not hit an iceberg!"

Towards the end of the time, Rosemary was interviewed separately by three of the women on the panel. They asked some unsettling questions, including what she would do if David were appointed as General Director – and then she found that there was no set role for her. She found this particularly upsetting as they had said they wanted a married couple. We had always sought to work together, whether in a church or mission, or on the staff of a college. Rosemary knew she could continue teaching courses at DTC or other colleges, or as the mission pastor at our Singapore church, but she wanted to be involved with OMF, working alongside me in ministry. As we caught the bus home after the interview, we both felt discouraged and were doubtful if we would be offered the job. To our surprise, we had a phone call that evening from David Pickard, saying that the interviewing panel was unanimous in recommending us for the role.

That was merely the beginning of the appointment process. First, all the field and home directors had to be consulted, and then, if they were all in agreement, all the members of OMF International worldwide were to be consulted. I assumed that did not include those who were now in heaven! The process lasted three months, until at last our appointment, or rather, to be more accurate, *my* appointment, was confirmed. I add that comment because, as we soon realised, although the mission had asked for a married couple they were actually looking for a married man. They had not thought through what the role of his wife should be if she were a Bible teacher like Rosemary, rather than a doctor, as was the case with Sue Pickard, wife of the outgoing general director, who could serve as a medical adviser.

In September 2001, fifty leaders of OMF came together at an international council meeting in Singapore. They came from the seventeen countries in Asia where OMF was working and the fourteen countries from which OMF missionaries were sent. A number of key issues were addressed and important decisions made. In particular, it was agreed that in future any position of leadership within the mission would be decided on the basis of gift and call rather than gender. Members of the council renewed their commitment to plant indigenous churches that were biblical in their teaching, contextualised in their expression of faith and worship, and eager to reach out to others with the gospel. They also expressed the desire to work closely with the national churches of Asia and to welcome an increasing number of Asians into the membership of OMF.

After two weeks of consultation, a service was held to bid farewell to David and Sue Pickard and to induct me as the ninth general director of OMF International. The service was held at St John's–St Margaret's church, and was attended by the Anglican bishop of Singapore, Dr John Chew; the principal of TTC, Dr Robert Solomon; and the vicar of the church, the Revd Rennis Ponniah. Dr Jim Taylor, the seventh general director and great-grandson of Hudson Taylor, also took part and handed me the Bible in which Hudson Taylor had written the words marking the beginning of the society: "Prayed for 24 willing, skilful labourers at Brighton June 25th 1865."

Steep learning curve

Prior to my induction, Rosemary and I had spent a week giving the Bible readings at the OMF field conference in Taiwan, arranged a long time before my appointment. At the suggestion of David Pickard, we flew on to Japan to visit the OMF team there. The day after we arrived in Tokyo, we caught the Shinkansen, or Japanese bullet train, from Tokyo to Sendai, where we were met by the leader of the small team working in that city. He promptly gave us leaflets and told us to post them through the letterboxes of the houses in nearby streets. We did not have a clue as to what was in the leaflets or whether what we were doing was legal. All went well until we reached a block of flats with a lobby containing multiple post boxes. As we started to put a leaflet in each one, an irate Japanese man came down the stairs and shouted at us in a most discouraging and threatening manner. We understood we were not meant to be doing what we were doing and retreated hastily. We had visions of my being imprisoned in Japan before I had even been inducted as general director!

On the return journey from Sendai, we were supposed to be met at Tokyo Station, but on arrival we saw no one we knew. Unsure what to do and not knowing a word of Japanese, we desperately looked round for a notice which might give us some information in English. We eventually found a huge board that appeared to give the price of tickets to every station in or near Tokyo. It was mainly in Japanese but there were a few names written in English, one of which was Ichikawa, which we knew was the station near the OMF office. We promptly purchased two tickets at the price shown on the board.

Our next challenge was to find the right platform. It is worth bearing in mind that this station is the busiest railway station in the world with 3.6 million people passing through every day. We tried to ask one or two people for help, pronouncing the name of Ichikawa as authentically as we could. Finally, someone pointed us down a very long corridor, which led to a small gate where a man was sitting with a timetable in a small booth. "Ichikawa?" we enquired hesitatingly. "No! No! No!" the man exclaimed. He then thumbed through his timetable and, after a while, said, "Funabashi! Change!"

Following his instructions, we found the train to Funabashi and then, with the help of a fellow traveller, found a connecting train to Ichikawa. At last, we arrived at our station and, with much relief, saw the wife of the home director there to meet us. But when we presented our tickets, the machine refused to let us go through the barrier. Puzzled, we turned to a ticket collector standing nearby. He looked at the tickets, then looked at us and scowled. He muttered something we did not understand and then waved us through. Our Japanese hostess looked at the tickets and smiled, "You bought tickets for children!"

Team leadership

My role as general director was to provide leadership for the mission, alongside four other international directors, who were very gifted and already well established in their roles. Ian Prescott, whom we knew well from his days as a student at All Nations, was international director for evangelism. Ian had served for twenty years in Asia and had a particular focus on the development of work in creative access contexts. He always brought fresh impetus to our evangelistic outreach and insightful comments to our meetings as directors. Patrick Fung, as international director for mobilisation, brought his invaluable insight and experience as a Chinese Christian who had served both as a missionary doctor in Pakistan and as home director in Hong Kong. Michael Littlefield and his wife LeMei had served for many years in Taiwan before he took up his post as international director for personnel. He had a warm heart, a deep pastoral care for people, and a fascination with the history of the American Civil War. Andrew Jackman, as international director for finance, brought great expertise to managing the business side of the mission through his experience in hospital administration in the UK NHS and serving as business manager for OMF in Central Thailand.

Working with such a team of younger colleagues was a huge privilege and made my task as general director so much easier. We met as often as possible as a group of directors and this enabled us to keep each other informed about significant developments. We were able to think through issues and crises as soon as they occurred. We also prepared the agenda for the six-monthly meeting of the International Executive Council when twelve leaders of the mission, each representing different aspects, met together in Singapore. Every two or three years a General Council of fifty or more leaders from all over the international OMF family met for a week to ten days for times of fellowship, prayer, and discussion. Through this leadership structure we were able to discuss and make decisions on the development of the international centre in Singapore, the reduction in mission costs, and the future vision for the mission.

With members working in virtually every country in East and Southeast Asia, as well as in many countries in the West, it was important to keep everyone informed about recent developments and plans. With the rapid advances in communication technology, it was becoming increasingly easy to send regular updates of mission news. I also began to record regular messages to the mission personnel on video, which could easily be sent to every country where we worked. I recorded some of these in the Botanic Gardens in Singapore and on one memorable occasion I stopped in the middle of a sentence to exclaim, "Look, there's a stork-billed kingfisher!"

During my first year as director I was able to visit China with Dr Jim Taylor, the great-grandson of Hudson Taylor. It was a privilege to make that visit with someone who knew China so well and who was a descendant of the founder of the mission. Dr Taylor and I visited one of the original stations of CIM where a minority ethnic group, in south-west China, were living as subsistence farmers. When a New Zealand sheep farmer, with the encouragement of Dr Taylor, came to this community, he was able to transform their lives by introducing improved stock and training local farmers in better husbandry. The farmer's work was so appreciated that he was offered honorary citizenship and invited to live permanently in China.

Rosemary was not able to accompany me on that trip to China because Ruth and her baby, Ryan, had become ill while she and Colin were working in a Christian hospital in North India. After less than a year, they came to us in Singapore to get medical treatment and to recover. It made Rosemary glad that she had not got a formal role with OMF, since she felt free to devote her attention to looking after them.

Mission in a changing world

Visiting one of the original mission stations of the China Inland Mission reminded me of the spiritual legacy of the mission with which we were now working. A few weeks earlier, I had carried a huge leather-bound volume from the mission archives to my office. It contained the record of all those who had served with CIM from the very beginning in 1865, giving the name, age, denomination, and profession of each new missionary candidate, stating when they sailed for China and when they died. The first name, hardly surprisingly, was that of James Hudson Taylor. The second was that of his wife, Maria. It was very moving to read through those records and be reminded of the dedication and sacrifice of so many who went to share the good news of Jesus with the people of China. One entry moved me to tears. It recorded the arrival of a 27-year-old missionary in Shanghai and then her death from typhoid a few months later.

In the nineteenth century, missionaries took months to sail from their home country to China. The standard length of the first term of service was seven years. There were no phones. Letters took a long time to arrive, if they arrived at all. Those who offered to go to China knew the cost of going was great. They would be separated from loved ones for many years and it was more than likely they would never see them again.

Life for the modern missionary is very different. Mission partners can travel from their home country to their country of service in less than a day. They are able to return home more frequently to renew contact with friends, family, and their local church. Those who pray for them can visit them in the places where they work and be in regular contact with them through phone calls, emails, Facebook, and video conferencing. While it was a great benefit to be so closely in touch with one's home country, those working overseas sometimes found it harder to concentrate on learning the local language and adapting to the surrounding culture. Within OMF, we had constantly to review the policies and practices of the mission in view of these changes.

Reaching out to those who have never heard

During the five years we served with OMF International, we were thrilled to witness the growth of the church in several countries in East Asia, like China, Cambodia, Mongolia, the Philippines, and Singapore. The rapid expansion of the church among mainland Chinese people seemed as remarkable as their economic development.

In 1989, the year that Mongolia obtained independence from the USSR, there were only a handful of Mongolian Christians. OMF began working there in 1992 under the auspices of an inter-agency association called Joint Christian Services, whose vision is "to see Mongolians building and restoring families, churches and communities". In the space of a few years, the number of believers increased and fellowships sprang up across the vast expanse of the Mongolian plateau. Bill Stephens, an OMF missionary, told us how one Mongolian Christian trekked for hundreds of miles to reach remote communities, preaching the good news and bringing Mongolians to faith. On one occasion, he returned to one community a year later to find that the Bible that he had given them had been read so often that it had almost disintegrated.

The mighty Mekong river, one of the longest rivers in Asia, flows for 2,500 miles from the Tibetan plateau through China's Yunnan province, Myanmar, Laos, Thailand, Cambodia, and Vietnam. On either side of the river, there are numerous ethnic groups, consisting of millions of people who have never had the opportunity to hear the good news. Fired by a vision to plant churches among these people, a group of OMF missionaries developed a strategic ministry among the unreached peoples who lived in the Mekong region.

With a flood of new candidates attracted to this ministry, teams focused on many minority groups and sought, after careful research, to discover the most effective way of reaching out to them with the gospel. This ministry expanded rapidly and with great vision and enthusiasm. An increasing number of people in different countries in Asia were beginning to work in cooperation and partnership with the mission. Sometimes these were people who were already working in an area where OMF was also at work. They wanted to be involved as much as possible but had not gone through the formal OMF channels of application and selection. Could they join OMF through the back door, as it were? Could they become associate members of the mission and what would that involve?

It takes time to change the policy of a mission with a history and traditions going back more than a hundred years. Some of our more zealous members who were anxious to get on with the task of reaching the unreached, with whoever wanted to work with them, began to get frustrated at the slow pace of change. The suggestion was made that they should leave OMF as a group and start a new mission unfettered by the traditions and policies of the past. This probably posed the most serious problem in my time as director. I immediately invited two of the leaders from the area to come to Singapore to talk and pray through the relevant issues with myself and other directors. In the event we were able to listen to one another and move forward as a united mission, grateful to those who had a burden to preach to those who had never heard and who were leading us forward into new frontiers of mission.

Challenges and opportunities

Political, economic, and social change have brought great challenges and opportunities to the Christian church and its mission. As many countries became closed to missionaries because of the rise of communism and the resurgence of other religions, Christians have discovered they could use professional qualifications to serve in these countries. While they might not be able to share their faith overtly, they could seek to be a witness in private conversation and, hopefully, through their lives. The range of professional skills that can be used to serve nations and communities is almost limitless. One country, which did not welcome evangelists or church planters, was advertising for lawyers, accountants, university lecturers, and English teachers. Architecture, mechanical engineering, stained-glass making, and sheep-farming are just a few examples of the wide range of skills and qualifications used by Christians to serve in countries that do not issue missionary visas. Within OMF, we realized that another way of serving a community was to start one's own company. Missional business was opening new doors of opportunity for members of the mission to make a difference in the lives of people and societies – spiritually, economically, socially, and environmentally.

The widespread acceptance of English as a universal language has led to a huge demand for English teachers all over the world, creating unprecedented openings for committed Christians to work and witness in countries that would otherwise be closed to them. I vividly remember watching one of our members, who was Chinese, teaching an English class in a communist country. The theme of the class was Christmas and the teacher asked his class of thirty sixteen-year-olds what words they associated with Christmas. "Presents," said one. "Father Christmas," said another. "Christmas carols," called out a third. The teacher then played the carol "Joy to the world, your Lord has come" on his guitar and, much to my amazement, all the children in the class knew the words and began to sing it. The teacher explained the meaning of the song and why some people believe that Jesus is the Lord of the world. I never expected to hear such a conversation in a secular school in an atheist country.

The massive movement of people around the world was also bringing new challenges and opportunities to us as a mission. By the year 2000, the number of international migrants globally had reached nearly 200 million. Many of these came from countries in Asia where they had less opportunity to hear the gospel. As some of our members who had worked in Asia returned home, they were able to continue their ministry among these migrant populations. Ministry among such communities and the many students who came to study in the West became an increasing priority within OMF. Having been involved in ministry among Jewish people in the UK, particularly among students, I was aware of the importance and potential of this ministry.

One of the most tragic events of my time with OMF demonstrated the value of Christians doing all they can to help those in need. In December 2004, a tsunami in the Indian Ocean hit the coast of several countries of South and Southeast Asia, causing immense destruction and loss of life. Thousands of Thai people died. Christians were among the first to provide aid and comfort. In one of the worst-hit areas, two OMF missionaries, Wikie and Elke, who knew the language and the culture, felt moved by a God-given compassion and a strong sense of his call to do what they could to help. They were not able to offer much in terms of financial assistance, but helped people restore their homes and rebuild their lives. In answer to a request from a Thai pastor, they spent hours listening as people shared their grief. They found it exhausting to listen intensely and empathetically to one tragic story after another. Thai Buddhists found it hard to do that because they feared that the obviously bad karma of the tsunami victims would affect their own karma and take away their own inner peace. As Christians, we can show the love and compassion of God, and share the good news of eternal peace that Jesus brings. The local people were deeply affected by the love shown by these two missionaries and others like them. They were grateful when they offered to pray for them, and their action led many to be drawn to the Saviour they followed. Within a short while, there were twenty-five small fellowships of new believers in that part of Thailand.

The internationalising of mission

A hundred years ago, mission agencies only accepted candidates from the West, but slowly attitudes began to change. In 1965, the OMF council decided to welcome Asian Christians into the mission, not just as the wives of Western missionaries, but as missionaries in their own right. By the time I became director in 2001, there were more than 300 Asian missionaries serving with the mission and an increasing number of these were Asians, now living in the West. They had heard God's call to return to Asia to share the gospel and strengthen the church. On a visit to Los Angeles, we met hundreds of Asian Christians with a similar burden for the continent, praying fervently for the spiritual needs of North Korea.

With an increasing number of missionaries across the world coming from Asia, Africa, and Latin America, many are being sent out directly by their home churches or through numerous indigenous mission agencies. Some join traditional missions from the West, like OMF, but they soon discover that it is not easy for Christians from these areas to join an international mission that has a predominantly Western ethos. Two years before I became general director, Rosemary Aldis, who had served as director for personnel for OMF in Singapore, conducted a survey among seventy Asian members of OMF, inviting them to share their experiences as Asians serving with an international mission. They explained that language was the greatest barrier and that, even if they were reasonably fluent in the use of English, they found it hard to participate in discussions of mission policy when native speakers seemed to talk so quickly. This often left them feeling excluded and convinced that fellow missionaries were not interested in their opinions. Several of them said they had encountered attitudes of racial or cultural arrogance among some missionaries, who appeared to have prejudice against or a sense of superiority over Asians.

These comments reminded me of other occasions when we had noticed a lack of cultural sensitivity on the part of some Christians from the West. While attending a conference in Nigeria, organised by the AEAM, Rosemary and I were shocked to hear a Western missiologist, who had not even visited Africa before, telling highly respected and experienced African leaders how to evangelise the continent. The leaders listened graciously but said nothing. Later, I asked one why he listened without responding. "Why didn't you challenge what he was saying?" I asked. To which he replied, "I might as well know what they are thinking because this is what they will send their missionaries to do." I then asked another leading mission trainer what he thought of the various strategies for world evangelisation that emanate from the West. "Do you really want to know?" he asked. "So much evangelical toxic waste!"

As national churches flourish and grow it is appropriate for them to have an increasing say in the evangelism within their own country and the work of mission in surrounding countries. We realised that within OMF there was a danger that those with a passion to share the gospel can continue to develop their mission strategies with little or no reference to local Christians or the national church. I sought to stress the importance of working in cooperation with local churches throughout my time as the head of the mission. I invited both the Anglican and the Methodist bishops in Singapore to attend my induction. In the light of the huge task facing the church in seeking to share the gospel with every individual and to plant a church in every community, it is imperative that churches and mission agencies work closely together.

I often wrestled with the question as to how far an international mission agency like ours was willing to adapt to the changes taking place in our world. How closely were we prepared to work in partnership with national churches, and how many national church leaders were we willing to appoint to our boards? Were we willing to change our ethos and become more culturally diverse? How far will our members be ready to use the language of the country in which they serve for their discussions on policy or times of worship? How quickly will we encourage our members from the Majority World to take over the leadership of the mission? As I approached the time of my retirement, I realised that the time was ripe for OMF to appoint an Asian Christian as my successor.

New missionaries and martyrs

My experience of the next generation of Asian missionaries in my time as director strengthened this conviction. In South Korea, we spent several days with forty Korean mission and church leaders, who were engaged in preparing Koreans for mission overseas. In Indonesia, we spoke at a conference for hundreds of university students who were keenly interested in the possibility of serving as missionaries. On the last night of the conference, many of them came forward to offer themselves for mission service. Along with others, we were asked to come to the front to counsel these students. Unfortunately, we found ourselves standing right in front of a huge loudspeaker that was blasting out "holy" music. The result was we could not hear a word being said by those who had come forward. So, we had to pray as best as we could and trust the Holy Spirit to interpret for us.

In OMF, we sought to encourage indigenous missionary movements. We welcomed more and more Asians to join the Fellowship and launched national mission agencies in Indonesia and the Philippines. Looking back to our time at All Nations, I longed to see the establishment of more Asian mission training centres which offered holistic preparation for cross-cultural service, adapted to the specific needs of the cultural context in which candidates would serve.

Within OMF there was such an increase in the number of candidates that we needed to add a fourth orientation course a year to provide training for them. The number of Asian candidates continued to grow to the point where they began to outnumber those coming from other backgrounds.

One of the most moving experiences during my time as general director was attending the funeral service of a young Filipino, Reuel, who served as a missionary with Serve Philippines, the daughter mission of OMF International. Reuel was only twenty-seven years old and his wife, Theresa, twenty-four. They had a two-year-old daughter, called Rejoice. For four years they had lived and worked in a predominantly Muslim town in Mindanao, in southern Philippines, seeking to demonstrate the love of God through their lives. Some people threatened to harm them and at one point they discussed with their team leaders whether they should leave the town and go to a safer place. As they prayed, they became convinced they should stay where they were. Some months later, Reuel was shot in the head as he leaned over his motorbike in the street. His murderer was a masked gunman, who stretched out his body in the form of a cross, as if to mock the faith that Reuel sought to represent. That was how Theresa found her husband's body.

Ten days later his funeral was held in a small gospel chapel on the mountainside. It was pouring with rain as his father, a Pentecostal pastor, led the service. Theresa spoke through her tears of her love and admiration for her husband. A friend was holding their daughter near the coffin of her father. "Where is your daddy?" she asked the little girl. In reply, Rejoice pointed her finger not towards the coffin but towards the sky. "He is with Jesus," she said.

The future of the Christian church in Asia rests with Asian Christians, men and women like Reuel and Theresa, who are deeply committed to Christ and determined that everyone should have an opportunity to hear the good news. The future of an international mission like OMF lies in its ability to respond to new challenges and opportunities and the extent to which it can work alongside national churches and missions.

Chapter 11
Re-tyred

In 2015, David spoke at the 10th international conference of LCJE in Jerusalem, where he met Meheretie, who taught him Amharic in Begemder over 40 years ago!

Those who hope in the Lord will renew their strength. They will soar on wings like eagles...

Isaiah 40:31

I had agreed to serve with OMF International until my sixty-fifth birthday in 2006. As the search began for my successor, it seemed the right time to seek for an Asian to lead the mission. After much prayer and due consideration, Dr Patrick Fung was appointed. He had already served for many years as one of the international directors and had previously worked with his wife Jennie in Pakistan where they both served as medical doctors. His experience in frontline mission together with his involvement in the management of the Hong Kong home side had given him a broad understanding of different aspects of the mission's work. His knowledge of both Cantonese and Mandarin, together with his understanding of China, would be an invaluable asset to the development of the mission. At a time when many still assume, even today, that leadership in world mission should remain in the hands of the Western church, we rejoice that God had provided for OMF such an experienced and deeply spiritual leader. It enabled Rosemary and myself to move on towards retirement, leaving the mission in capable hands.

Throughout our ministry, we have been very conscious of God's goodness to us. What a privilege it has been to be challenged and inspired by Christian brothers and sisters all over the world. We have had the opportunity to share from God's Word in many different countries. Rosemary has often said that when she accepted my proposal of marriage, agreeing to go anywhere in the world to serve the Lord, she did not realise that would mean going everywhere!

At several critical points in our lives, God guided us in a clear way, helping us to know his will. At other times we were asked to do things that did not immediately seem the right way forward, but God gave us peace and, in time, we understood how they were part of his plan. On occasions, we were faced with a choice between equally plausible possibilities and we had to weigh up what was right. We now look back and are amazed to see how God has been with us all the way, as he promises in Proverbs 3:5–6. "Trust in the Lord with all your heart and lean not on your own understanding; in all your ways submit to him and he will make your paths straight."

God's provision

Throughout our lives, we have experienced God's provision. The Lord has been our shepherd and, although being in Christian ministry does not usually result in a large salary, we have never lacked anything we needed. In the years when we returned from Ethiopia and worked with CMJ in London, our allowance just covered our needs. When our son Andrew was about ten years old, he was concerned about what would happen if we both died. "We would not have enough money to bury you," he said. "We would have to put you in a dustbin and roll you down the hill." A charming thought! A few years later, he was able to write and sell computer programs, which meant he had more money in the bank than we had ever had.

As we got older, we were left money by our parents and kind aunts, and were able to invest in a small flat in London. One day in 2003, the day before we were due to fly back to Singapore, a friend rang us up to ask if we had read the *Daily Telegraph* that day. She explained that it contained a notice from a solicitor, which read: "Would Rosemary Harley, nee Holder...please contact our office where she will learn something to her advantage." Her parents had both died by then and her other relatives were all very much alive. She could not imagine who could have left her any money. When she contacted the solicitor, she was surprised to find that her godfather, whom she had not seen for many years and whom she assumed had died long ago, had named her in his will. With his legacy, we were able to sell our flat and buy a house in Exeter for our retirement.

Why Exeter? Three years before we retired from OMF, we were both preaching at St Leonard's Church in Exeter. At the end of the evening service, the vicar asked us where we were going to live in retirement. "Why not come to Exeter?" he suggested. "We could make use of you at St Leonard's." A year later, we were back in the UK again, speaking on behalf of OMF. This allowed us a few days to look at possible properties in Exeter. The second house we saw, which we had viewed online from Singapore, was very suitable, so we offered the asking price. Other potential buyers, who saw the house immediately after us, tried to gazump us, but the owners refused their higher offer. This all happened in four days and we were again so grateful to God for his provision.

We enjoyed that house for eight years until the beginning of 2014 when Rosemary suffered severe heart failure while we were in Southeast Asia. Since it was a three-storey house on a very steep hill, we decided it was time for us to move into a bungalow. We were dreading the long and drawn-out process of selling our house and buying a new home. The one bungalow we liked was too expensive, much more than we expected to get for our house. Then, amazingly, the price for the bungalow was dropped and the estate agent set a much higher price for our house than we had expected. Even before the details of our house were put on the Internet, a man made an offer that matched the revised price of the bungalow. We accepted his offer, and the next morning we heard that our offer on the bungalow had been accepted. We were able to move within two months, to the amazement of ourselves and the surprise of friends, who had spent two years trying to move house.

New avenues of service

In March 2006, I was delighted to pass the baton of leadership to Patrick Fung as the first Asian general director of OMF International. For me, it had been an immense privilege to lead a mission founded nearly 150 years before as the China Inland Mission, to work with amazing colleagues and to witness the dedication of those who joined the mission. We visited OMF personnel in sixteen out of the seventeen countries of East Asia where they worked. We sought to listen to them as they shared their hopes and concerns, and to encourage them from the Scriptures as we spoke at their annual conferences. We were never sure whether we had been any help when we visited them, but invariably as we left, we were glad to be told, "You have been such an encouragement."

OMF colleagues arranged a dinner to say goodbye. Our church cell group also organised a superb Chinese dinner with all our favourite dishes. The mission department and staff of the church also gave us a special lunch with a European menu to prepare us for reverse culture shock. In the last two weeks, we had numerous meals with friends and colleagues. We thank God for the privilege of working with such wonderful colleagues and belonging to such an encouraging church.

During the first three months back, we travelled around the UK speaking on behalf of the mission and visiting prayer supporters. The tenants in our house moved out in June and we stayed with Ruth and her family, while we painted some of the rooms and bought a bed! Ruth and Colin were living in Exeter with their children, Ryan and Emma, and we were looking forward to being close to part of our family after ten years based in Singapore. We were only sad that Exeter is a long way from London, where Andrew and Jean were living with their three boys, and where Catherine was working as a web designer for the department store John Lewis.

When we first went to Ethiopia with a very young family, several people warned us that taking our small children to live in a remote part of Africa might interfere with their education and limit their opportunities in life. We subsequently heard stories of the children of missionaries who turned against their parents' faith. We are grateful to God that this did not happen and their experience seemed to enrich their understanding of the world and their appreciation of other cultures. Their education did not suffer. All three went through university, and then pursued careers in IT, education, and the Arts. Andrew is managing director of Give Clarity, a team of experienced charity professionals whose mission is to help charities and social enterprises in their fundraising and supporter relationships. Ruth is a lecturer and a race equality resource officer at the University of Exeter, and is completing a PhD. Catherine, formerly a web designer, who also worked at Christian charity Interserve, more recently studied acting at East 15 and is now working as an actor while writing a script based on a missionary's life.

In Exeter, I was glad to be free from administration and responsibility, but moving from full-time work to "retirement" brings its own challenges. For many years, I had been engaged in discussing strategy and providing leadership. Now it was the turn of other people to assume those responsibilities, and it felt strange not to be involved any longer. Similarly, while we had been living in Singapore, we had constant invitations to speak in churches and at conferences, but on our return to the UK, such invitations were few and far between. I had always known that if I looked for my sense of identity in a particular position or in public recognition, I would be disappointed. The process of discovering that no one is interested in your opinion any more can still be painful, until we remember our value is and always has been in the fact that we are loved children of God, and that is in no way diminished by the fact that we are no longer in the public eye, doing "significant things".

It was not long before we discovered that retirement does not mean a life of ease. It simply marks the beginning of a new stage in life, an opportunity, not to stop, but to be re-tyred for further service, albeit at a slower pace. Before we left Singapore in April, we were very grateful to have already received an invitation to teach an MA course at Singapore Bible College in October and to have invitations to speak at conferences, churches, and other Bible colleges. In the following years, I supervised doctoral theses, while we both facilitated postgraduate courses on contextualisation and helped facilitate weeklong Langham preaching seminars for pastors in Thailand and Myanmar.

We enjoyed speaking at mission conferences, where we sought to listen to people as they shared their experiences and to encourage them from God's Word. We were helped by having worked with three different missions in a variety of ministries and cultural contexts to apply biblical truth to issues and challenges faced by missionaries in today's world.

During our retirement, we were sometimes asked to speak on a specific theme or from a particular book of the Bible, but often the choice of topic or biblical passages was left up to us. Invited to address one conference I suggested speaking on the life of Elisha. One of the area directors responded that he did not see how that would be relevant to the members of his team. I was shocked that a leader might think that any part of God's Word lacked relevance to him and his co-workers, and I was determined to show how the Scriptures can speak in relevant ways in every situation. I wrote to several team leaders, asking them what were their particular struggles and challenges. They replied in great detail, telling me of the trials and difficulties they were encountering in their ministry. I then sought to relate the studies from the life of Elisha to those issues. Afterwards, the leader who had been sceptical said with appreciation, "But it was all so relevant!"

We were helped in our retirement by having more time to prepare for different talks and seminars. Rather than being rushed off our feet with a plethora of things crying out for our attention, we could focus for many weeks on a particular sermon or conference. The result was we became more prayerful about each event and could think more about the people who would be listening and the issues they might be facing.

There were several times when I was aware God was speaking in a special way. One was at a retreat for the clergy of the Anglican diocese of Singapore. I had been invited by Bishop Rennis Ponniah, who had been our pastor previously. There were more than a hundred clergy together for four days and we looked at the role of the pastor-shepherd through the life of Moses. We had five hour-long sessions in which we were able to study the life of this great leader of God's people. Bishop Rennis led the sessions sensitively, allowing time for each person to reflect and listen to what God was saying to them.

At the end of one session, when we had reflected on the disobedience of Moses in Numbers 20, there was a moving time when a brother sought forgiveness from all those present for serious failure in his life, for which he had been disciplined and removed from ministry for three years. He spoke for half an hour with humility and sincerity of the ways in which he had let down his family, his congregation, and his fellow clergy. As he concluded, he was warmly embraced by those present and welcomed back into ministry. It was a striking example of how discipline within the church can be exercised appropriately, lovingly and effectively.

From player to coach

During her time as mission pastor at SJSM, Rosemary encouraged several members of the church as they responded to God's call to missionary service. It was a period in the life of the church when a significant number felt called to serve God in Thailand, Laos, and China. It was good to belong to a church involved in the growing Asian missionary movement, and Rosemary was anxious to help in any way she could. Since we retired, we have kept in touch with many of them and, as our speaking engagements and travel allowed we visited them in the countries where they were serving. We had always visited former students on our travels, but now in retirement, we had more time to visit students from All Nations, DTC, and TTC, as well as mission partners from SJSM. We saw it as a great privilege to support and encourage the next generation of workers.

In Exeter, we discovered a group of people at St Leonard's Church who were all sensing God's call to use their gifts overseas. We sought to stress the importance of being properly trained before they went and suggested they might go to All Nations for one or two years. It soon became apparent that for one reason or another they were unable to do so at that time. We then realised we could provide some level of training through using the Perspectives Course.[1] We had five people, meeting once a month for fifteen months, and studying the recommended reading. This group, which seemed to be brought together by God, had a significant impact on the lives of those who attended. The married couple went to Kenya and we have been able to visit them twice and speak at the annual conference of their mission. Two others got engaged and married, then went to serve in Senegal. The other member of the group was the secretary of the church mission committee.

When we moved to Trinity Church, which was nearer our new home on the edge of Exeter, there were five gifted mission partners, two couples serving with OMF, and Emma Brewster, working with SIM in South Africa. We already knew Steve and Anna Griffiths because we had worked with them in Singapore when they were international directors for personnel. We soon got to know the other couple, Rich and Zoe, who were working in Asia. When they returned on home assignment, I enjoyed meeting up with Rich on a regular basis for mutual encouragement. When they are back in Asia, we can continue to meet up and chat online. There are others, engaged in ministry in other parts of the UK, who appreciated having times when we could share and pray together. Again, I felt this was a privilege and was grateful that in our late seventies God still had work for geriatrics to do!

Coping with the unexpected

When Rosemary experienced severe heart failure in January 2014, we were on a trip to Thailand. We had visited a national park with the SJSM missionary with whom Rosemary had worked closely in Singapore, and we had also spent time with Thai friends who had been students at DTC. On the last two days of our visit, Rosemary's legs began to hurt and she became unable to walk more than 25 yards. When we got to the airport in Bangkok to fly to Singapore, she had to use a wheelchair. On arrival in Singapore, we rang Steve Griffiths, a medical doctor, who was still working at OMF International headquarters in Singapore. He urged us to go as quickly as possible to the emergency department at the hospital nearby.

Although it was very late at night, the doctor on duty fetched a vascular specialist and a cardiologist to examine Rosemary, and admitted her to the high dependency unit (HDU). Her heart had three major problems: irregular heartbeats had sent small clots to the arteries of her lower legs; her right and left ventricles were not synchronised; and she had sick sinus syndrome, which meant her own heart's natural pacemaker was not working as it should. Fortunately, an MRI scan and an angiogram revealed no other problems.

When the cardiologist could not steady her heart rate with medication, he decided it was necessary to implant a three-lead pacemaker (CRTD). That proved a difficult procedure and the specialist had problems attaching one of the leads to her heart even after several attempts. Just as the surgeon was about to give up, he found another vein in which to insert the lead. It seemed to have been a successful procedure but the following morning when he visited Rosemary in the HDU he realised things were not working properly and said, "I am very worried." Rosemary was kept under observations for a further day but by then everything seemed to be functioning correctly. I had sent round an urgent request for prayer and we know many people were praying for her at that time. We were extremely grateful that God so graciously answered those prayers. Rosemary was then able to leave the hospital to begin the process of convalescence. The specialist set off for China for a lecture tour where he said he was going to use the problems he had with Rosemary's surgery as a case study!

Medical treatment in Singapore is of the very highest standard, but it is not cheap. Rosemary's hospital bill came to over £40,000. As we had travel insurance, the company covered virtually all the costs and, in the end, we only had to contribute the princely sum of £40. In addition, when we returned to the UK, the company rang up to ask how many nights Rosemary had spent in hospital. They said, "We would like to pay her £50 for each night she suffered from the inconvenience of being in hospital." They later sent us a cheque for £700. I asked Rosemary why she did not stay in hospital longer!

All the time Rosemary was in hospital, a family from SJSM looked after me, often driving me early in the morning to the hospital door. Wey Fook and Priscilla Hou and their four children are a very hospitable family, who had invited us to stay with them on many previous visits to Singapore. They have a large house on three storeys, and had designed the top floor with three extra en-suite bedrooms so they could welcome missionaries and visiting preachers. This time they made their guest room on the ground floor available to us when Rosemary came out of hospital, as her dead heart muscle means she cannot walk up many stairs. There was no need for us to shop, cook, clean, or wash clothes. Everything was done for us. How grateful we are to this family. What a wonderful example of Christian hospitality!

While Rosemary was in hospital and, later, when she returned home, a continuous stream of visitors came from OMF International and SJSM. Former colleagues from DTC visited her and, in spite of his busy schedule, Bishop Rennis came to pray with her three times. Again, how grateful we are to God for his mercy and provision, and to friends who showed us so much love and care.

It took time for Rosemary to recover and she is still restricted in what she can do, but that same year she helped me lead a Master of Theology seminar in Malaysia and we did a month's speaking tour of New Zealand, where her sessions on witnessing to people of other faiths were particularly popular. The next few years saw us speaking in Thailand, Israel, Singapore, Hong Kong, Myanmar, Denmark, and Germany. Rosemary was also invited to speak at Keswick in Devon, while I became involved in leading extension courses for Moorlands College. We both spoke fairly regularly in our local church and shared in the leadership of a home group. It may sound as though we were very busy, but this was all spread over several years and we never felt under too much pressure. At the same time, we are aware that as we get older it is wise to avoid long-distance travel if possible and concentrate on more local ministry.

While we no longer travel far, many friends, former students, and colleagues have come to visit us. We live in the south-west corner of the UK, a popular holiday destination famed for its beautiful countryside, great beaches and warm climate. Our home lies within a mile of the motorway used by holidaymakers travelling to Devon and Cornwall. We are glad when friends take the opportunity to visit us instead of the nearby service station. We are greatly encouraged by fellowship with these visitors, as we hear how they are serving God.

We have sometimes been asked why we spent our lives in missionary service and why we were willing to make many sacrifices.

An Indian lady who managed the hotel near our house in Mek'ele, once asked me why I had wasted my life in Ethiopia. "You could have had a proper job and earned lots of money," she said. We never thought in those terms. We did not feel we had made any sacrifices or thrown away opportunities for more exciting careers. In fact, we cannot imagine a life more enjoyable or fulfilling than the one we have had.

Chapter 12
Model for Mission

Silas and Marcia Tostes, who were students during
David's time as principal at ANCC are now training
Brazilian missionaries to serve all over the world

*After this the Lord appointed seventy[1] others, and sent them
on ahead of him, two by two, into every town and place
where he himself was about to come. And he said to them, "The
harvest is plentiful, but the labourers are few; pray therefore
the Lord of the harvest to send out labourers into his harvest."*

Luke 10:1–2, RSV

When invited to speak on mission, I have frequently preached on Luke 10, where Jesus sends a large group of disciples ahead of him into the villages around Galilee. This chapter of the Bible provides an appropriate starting point to discuss the nature and practice of mission. It shows the vision Jesus had for a great harvest, the kind of people he sent out, the task he gave them to do, and the conditions in which they were to carry out that task. I also appreciate these verses because they reflect so many of the lessons we have learned as we have tried to follow and serve Jesus.

It must have been a surprise for the seventy disciples when they were told by Jesus to go out and preach. They had been happy to follow him around, listening to his teaching. They were amazed to see him perform one miracle after another and then they were surprised to be told they were to go out and do the same! An early lesson they had to learn was that if they were going to be followers of Jesus, they were called to action. Being a disciple of Jesus is not simply a matter of listening to his teaching. It means going out into the world to minister to peoples' needs and to announce the coming of God's kingdom.

The vision Jesus has

As Jesus prepares them for their mission, he tells them: "The harvest is plentiful". He anticipates a harvest of people, ready to respond to the message of hope, forgiveness, acceptance, purpose, and healing that he brings. Initially, he sends this group of disciples to villages around Galilee so they can learn what it will mean to be involved in his mission to the world. After the day of Pentecost, Jesus sent his followers in the power of the Holy Spirit to reach not just a few villages in Galilee but every nation of the world. It is significant that Jesus chooses to send out seventy, because in contemporary Jewish thought seventy was the number of the nations of the world.

That's the vision of Jesus. That's God's vision as revealed through the whole of scripture. The story of the Bible is the story of God's love for the world. God made the world and cares for all those he has created. He called Abraham to be a blessing to all the nations of the earth. He chose Israel to be a light to the nations. He sent his Son to be the Saviour of the world. He sent his Spirit that the gospel might be taken to the nations. At the end of time, he will gather people from all the nations. This is the vision of Jesus.

Both Rosemary and I had felt, when we were still young, that we should play a part in God's desire to bless the world. We realised that God calls every Christian to care for others and share the good news with all people. We began our ministry together with a strong focus on the Jewish people, serving among the Falasha Jews of Ethiopia and the Jewish community in the UK. When we were invited to join the staff of All Nations College, we sensed God was calling us to have a wider vision, a vision for all nations. Around that time, I was invited to preach at a church in Bath about the blessings we had received from the Jewish people and the good news of the Messiah that we could share with them. As I sat in the church before the service, I looked up at the beautiful stained-glass window at the east end of the building. It was a picture of Jesus, surrounded by his disciples, saying to them, "Go and make disciples of all nations" (Matthew 28:19). We had already felt God saying this to us and seeing these words confirmed to us that we should indeed go to All Nations! It would enable us to help men and women from different countries and continents to go all over the world to make disciples. In time, we too were able to visit many of those countries and be inspired by the witness of dedicated Christians and the rapid growth of the universal church.

In Kenya, we were blessed by meeting Christians, relatively poor by Western standards, yet exhibiting a radiant joy and deep trust in the Lord Jesus. We were challenged by the life of an evangelist in Tanzania, who moved from village to village sharing the gospel, carrying only his cooking pot, his spear, his blanket, and his Bible. Small wonder the church in sub-Saharan Africa grows so fast. African Christians are leading Africans to Christ. In the 1950s, the church in Africa was so small, some observers predicted that it might soon disappear completely, overwhelmed by the forces of Marxism, Islam, and nationalism. Today there are more than 600 million Christians in Africa and it is rapidly becoming a global centre of the Christian faith. Even in London, the decline in the number of those attending church has been reversed through the growth of African- and Asian-led churches.

One of the greatest privileges of my life was addressing a thousand Chinese pastors and seeking to encourage them from the Scriptures. This amazing group of men and women were evidence of the huge growth of the Church in China. Before Mao Tse Tung proclaimed the People's Republic of China in 1949, there were fewer than a million Protestant Christians in China. Today, no one is sure how many Christians there are, but estimates vary from 70 million to more than 100 million.

It is encouraging to hear of the growth of the church in Africa and China, and to know that similar growth is taking place in many other countries. In the UK, we witness decline in church attendance and some churches being closed or sold to become warehouses or restaurants or even mosques. For many Christians in the UK the critical question is not "Can we grow?" but "Can we survive?" It is encouraging then for them to have a global perspective. Jesus is still gathering his harvest. He is building his church and the gates of hell will not prevail against it (Matthew 16:18).

While this is a source of comfort and reassurance, there is no room for complacency. It is great to hear that there are so many Christians in China, but the fact remains that there are more than a billion people in China who do not know Christ. Among the 126 million Japanese, less than 2 per cent are Christians. The church in Thailand is very small. Among the 60 million Thai people, less than 1 per cent believe in Jesus. We visited one university in Thailand where not a single student knew anything about Jesus.

When we visited Northwest China, former All Nations students drove us over a rough road through barren countryside to a remote Tibetan town, where there was a large temple complex. As we watched people repeatedly turning the prayer wheels on the walls of the temple, we noticed a poorly clad woman walking slowly around the whole temple area. She took a pace forward and then prostrated herself on the ground. After a moment of silent prayer, she stood up and took another forward step before prostrating herself on the ground again. She kept repeating this ritual, and we realised that it would take her many hours to go around the large complex. We wondered what pain or sorrow was in her heart, what urgent need drove her to such desperate prayer. To what god or spirit was she praying? We longed to tell her of her heavenly Father who loved her and listened to the cry in her heart.

There are so many in our contemporary world who have never heard the gospel in ways they can understand. They have never realised they can call the creator of the world their Father. They have never experienced the peace that comes because Jesus died on the cross. They have never known the joy of the Spirit in their hearts and they have no sure hope of eternal life.

A year or so ago, I gave a week's teaching on the book of Exodus to thirty young pastors and evangelists in a country in North Africa. Each of them came from a Muslim background and it was heart-warming to hear their stories of how they came to personal faith in Jesus. In his book *Wind in the House of Islam*,[2] David Garrison has recorded stories of nine areas of the world, in each of which there has been a significant movement of at least 1,000 Muslims coming to personal faith in Jesus. Yet there are still more than one billion Muslims who know nothing of God's love for them, shown in the death of his son.

Jesus had a vision of a great harvest, an ingathering of people from all over the world who would accept his love, his forgiveness and his salvation. He calls each of us to play our part in realising that vision and commands us to pray that God will send out more workers to gather the harvest: "The harvest is plentiful, but the labourers are few; pray therefore the Lord of the harvest to send out labourers into his harvest" (Luke 10:2, RSV).

The people Jesus uses

We are told little about this group of disciples that Jesus sends out in Luke 10. They are simply referred to as "others". They were not apostles. They were not well known. Their names are not even recorded. That is both salutary and encouraging: salutary because it prevents those of us who serve as pastors or missionaries from thinking we are special, encouraging because it means that God can use any of us, however unsuitable or inadequate we feel. Rosemary and I are aware of mistakes we have made, of opportunities we have wasted, of occasions when we have disappointed the Lord by our behaviour. Although we are grateful for the abilities he has given us, we are aware there are many more gifted and more effective in ministry. We are so grateful that God uses ordinary people. One of my favourite biblical passages is the one where Paul says, "Remember, dear brothers and sisters, that few of you were wise in the world's eyes or powerful or wealthy when God called you... As a result, no one can ever boast in the presence of God" (1 Corinthians 1:26, 29, NLT). Jesus does not use people because they are special or gifted. He does not use very holy people. He does not use super saints, because there aren't any. He uses ordinary people – "others".

Jesus sent the disciples out two by two. He knew they had not had much teaching and were limited in their understanding. He realised how easily they could become discouraged if they were sent out alone. While we admire those students who, having trained at All Nations, have served alone for decades in isolated and sometimes hostile environments, Rosemary and I have been so grateful that we have been able to work alongside each other, compensating the weakness of each by the strength of the other. One of the reasons we called this book "Together in Mission" is because we are aware that we could not have coped with the challenges and pressures of ministry by ourselves.

These seventy disciples seemed reluctant to become itinerant preachers. The strong verb used in verse 2 of Luke 10 implies that the Lord of the harvest had to compel the workers to go out.

The one thing that these disciples had in their favour was that they had been with Jesus. They had listened to his teaching, seen him perform miracles, and had ample opportunity to observe his life. In the case of the twelve apostles, Jesus spent three years with them, teaching them and training them before he sent them out into the wider world. We were grateful that although we had both studied theology and served in a church for three years, we were still able to spend a year at All Nations in preparation for our service in another continent. The fifteen years we spent on the staff at the college only served to heighten our conviction of the importance of thorough training and spiritual preparation for those who are going out into the world as Christ's ambassadors. I am as convinced as ever that those who feel called to reach out in cross-cultural evangelism and service should be fully prepared and trained before they go out. It seems the height of arrogance to assume that we don't need any substantial preparation. I remember a conversation with the leaders of one mission agency who were providing just two weeks' training to young people they were sending out as witnesses in the Middle East. How were those young people meant to share the gospel effectively with Muslims if they hardly knew the first thing about Islam? How were they to avoid making the most fundamental mistakes in their witness if they knew nothing of the past relationships between Christians and Muslims?

Jesus took time to prepare those he sent out and he began by letting them spend time with him – the foundation of Christian service for each of us is a relationship with Jesus. Whatever we seek to do in his name can only be effective if it stems from that relationship. But that is precisely where we so often fail. There is a danger among evangelicals that we can be so busy with our programmes, our strategies, our multiplicity of meetings and committees, that we fail to spend adequate time cultivating our relationship with God, listening to what he is saying to us. I can imagine that if Jesus spoke up at one of our committee meetings and said, "There is something I would like to discuss with you," the chair of the meeting might reply, "I am sorry, but that is not on the agenda." This danger of being preoccupied with our own ideas and ministries was brought home to me during a discussion with the leaders of a mission who were planning a retreat to spend time listening to God. One of their most ardent evangelists, who had a burning passion to reach the unreached, exclaimed they did not have time to hold a retreat. He implied the task of global evangelism was too urgent to "waste time" doing that!

The task Jesus assigns

When Jesus sends out these seventy disciples, he begins by commanding them to heal the sick – to care for the physical needs of those they meet. By the grace of God, they were able to perform miracles as Jesus did. After Jesus had returned to his Father, his followers continued to perform miracles and cared for people's physical needs in other ways. They looked after widows and collected money for famine victims, demonstrating the love of God in action. In so doing, they reflected the character of Jesus, for when he saw the sick, he healed them and when he saw the hungry, he fed them.

We live in a world of enormous physical needs, where 100 million children live on the streets of the world's cities, where 10 million children are forced into child prostitution, and where thousands of children die every day from malnutrition. As the followers of Jesus, we are called to be compassionate people, who show the love of God in action.

While other members of our small mission team in Ethiopia were involved in medical work, Rosemary and I were not initially involved in meeting people's physical needs. We had both felt called to teaching ministries and went to Ethiopia with the intention of being engaged in Bible teaching. Although we recognised the value of a good general education, we wanted to use our teaching abilities to explain the Scriptures. Our primary goal had been to teach in a Bible college in Africa, but this never happened. The one Bible school in which we might have been employed was closed soon after we arrived. Later, when we were moved to Mek'ele, we found ourselves teaching English, modern maths, and Ethiopian history.

We were able to give teaching on the Bible in a school founded to train Orthodox priests and offer some evening Bible classes. We greatly enjoyed these and they seemed to fit with our original goal, but our experience was a salutary reminder that those who go out to serve others need to be flexible and willing to adapt their own goals to the needs of the people and the opportunities God provides.

When there was a severe famine in Ethiopia in 1973, we did become closely involved in providing relief to the families of those who suffered. At times, the streets of the town of Mek'ele, where we lived, were filled with destitute families who had fled from the worst-hit areas and were seeking food and shelter. It was impossible to ignore the plight of fellow human beings and we were glad that the school, where we were teaching, was able to provide accommodation for 200 children orphaned by the famine. One of my more challenging tasks was working with Ethiopian colleagues to select the most deserving cases. At the same time Rosemary was able to link some of the poorest children, who were attending our school, with the foreign agencies who provided them with regular basic support.

Jesus did not just tell them to be involved in social action. He also commanded the seventy to announce that the kingdom of God had come. The disciples were called to preach a message of faith and repentance, and they were to preach to everyone, without exception. This wonderful message of grace is also a solemn message because of the consequences for those who reject it (Luke 10:10–12).

In John's Gospel, Jesus declares that he is the way, the truth, and the life, and no one comes to the Father but through him (John 14:6). Jesus is the king who makes it possible to enter the kingdom of God. He is the Saviour of the world. Such a claim sounds unpalatable in modern society and those who proclaim it are often regarded as arrogant. Yet, with humility and sensitivity, we are called to share what we do know and to proclaim the good news that the Saviour of the world has come. We have always tried to present this universal message in meaningful and relevant ways in different contexts. How we present the good news depends on the people to whom we are speaking. When Jesus spoke to Nicodemus, he spoke in terms of the kingdom. He used the theological language with which he was familiar as a scholar of the Hebrew Scriptures (John 3). But when he talks with the Samaritan woman, he speaks about finding fresh water. He uses an idiom from her daily life, an illustration she understands (John 4). That is the challenge we face. How do we present the wonderful message of eternal life in terms that people understand? "How shall they hear?" is the cry of Paul's heart. But his burden is not just that the message will be audible but that it will be understood.

As we study the New Testament letters, we see how Paul and Peter use one illustration after another, one analogy after another, to communicate the full meaning of Christ's death on the cross. Christ died for our sins, he redeems us from slavery, he washes us clean from sin, he sets us free from the power of the spirits, he makes us a holy people, he reconciles us to God and he gives us eternal life.

Paul trawls the Scriptures for suitable terms. He searches the secular world for apt illustrations from everyday life. His theology is always focused on the death and resurrection of Jesus, but he always seeks to explain the significance of his death in terms that his audience can understand. As Dean Flemming points out in his insightful book, *Contextualization in the New Testament*,[3] Paul is always audience-sensitive without being audience-driven. We too face the same challenge of making the message intelligible and meaningful to the people with whom we are talking.

For women, who in some communities have low self-esteem because they are treated as chattels, the gospel proclaims that through Jesus' death they can become daughters of God. For those who live in constant fear of the spirits, the gospel proclaims that Christ has conquered all the powers of evil and set them free. For those who are living in constant fear of unspeakable suffering beyond the grave, the gospel proclaims the hope of eternal life. For those burdened by the conviction that they must do something to earn their salvation, the gospel proclaims that Christ has done everything necessary. As we reach out in our pluralist society to the people of other cultures, we face the challenge of how to make the message of the kingdom and the message of the cross meaningful so that they hear and understand, repent and believe.

It is no simple task, and it is so easy to make mistakes and miscommunicate the gospel. I was reading the dissertation of a Chinese Christian, who lived in Singapore and had used the four spiritual laws, a simplified summary of the gospel, as an effective means of evangelism for many years. He saw many people come to Christ. He then went to live and work in China, using the same approach in his witness. After seven years, he concluded that his use of the four spiritual laws communicated the wrong message in that communist country. He was starting from belief in God in a society which denies the existence of God. He was speaking of sin which in Mandarin was understood as committing a crime. He spoke of prayer, which was interpreted as ancestor worship. He felt his whole approach was too aggressive in a society where building relationships was regarded with great importance, and that he had failed to contextualize his message and his method.

In Thailand, I know some enthusiastic Christians use John 3:16 to witness to their Thai Buddhist friends. The problem is that their friends misunderstand what they are saying. The Buddhist does not believe in God and assumes the Christian is talking about some lesser being belonging to the world of gods and spirits who has not reached the blessed state of Nirvana. The Christian speaks of God's love but for the Buddhist, emotions like love or desire do not provide the solution to the human condition. He believes that all our problems come from our desires. The Christian speaks of eternal life, but the Buddhist does not see this as good news, since he wants to escape from the never-ending cycle of reincarnation.

For many years, Rosemary used a presentation called "Chopsticks and Chips"[4] to help Christians understand how to communicate the gospel more effectively to people from diverse cultural backgrounds. She recommended they should follow six basic steps.

Firstly, **learn** as much as possible about the country, culture, and religion of the person they are seeking to reach. Secondly, **listen** to the people, using what you have learned to ask questions and to gain a personal understanding of the individual, as they share their hopes and concerns. Thirdly, **love** them by offering hospitality and practical help as appropriate. Fourthly, **live** a life that witnesses for Christ and shows the fruit of the Spirit. Fifthly, **look** for creative ways of overcoming barriers and building bridges of understanding. And finally, **lean** on the Lord in everything you seek to do to win these friends to Christ, continually praying for them and seeking his guidance and the work of his Spirit.

The demands Jesus makes

When Jesus sends out his disciples, he warns them that they will face suffering and danger. They will be vulnerable like lambs among wolves, who may tear them to pieces. Jesus never promises his followers an easy, comfortable, prosperous life, but warns them of opposition and persecution.

On one occasion we were speaking to a group of people working in Northeast China who had a burden for North Korea. Sadly, one of their colleagues, who had worked in North Korea for ten years, setting up three clinics, had then been arrested, imprisoned, and beaten up. The police had discovered that he had been sharing his faith with some North Koreans and that is absolutely forbidden. As we talked with these Christian workers, they were having to come to terms with the possibility they might have to face a similar ordeal.

For 2,000 years, Christians have suffered for their faith. Many who have tried to take the good news of Jesus to the far corners of the earth have paid the ultimate price. We should not be surprised, for this is what Jesus predicted, and we can never assume as followers of Christ we will be exempt from suffering. In our family we have not suffered physically and, although we had to adopt a simple lifestyle while living in rural Ethiopia, it never seemed a great hardship. One of the hardest things for us was being misunderstood by one or two of our friends and family members. Some questioned why we were throwing our lives away, while others disagreed in principle with the very concept of Christian mission.

Jesus told the disciples to live simply. They were not to take a purse or a bag or sandals. They were to accept whatever hospitality they were given. They were to make sacrifices and forgo some of their comforts. They were not to let their mission be hampered by concern about their possessions. It could be argued that this was a unique and relatively short campaign, so it does not provide a blueprint for long-term ministry. It still raises questions for every generation about our attitude to our possessions and what we are willing to give up in our service of Christ. God may challenge us to live more simply so that we can give more to others.

A further instruction Jesus gave to his disciples was to take care they do not become distracted along the way. They must be single-minded, having a clear focus on the task they have been given. Jesus gave the seventy specific places to go. He did not want them to be diverted on their journey by meeting some friend or family member and spending the day with them rather than fulfilling the task he had assigned.

Jesus calls us all to be willing to suffer, to live simply and to be single-minded, and he has set us an example. He left his father's throne, gave up his glory and came to earth, born as a man, born to a humble family, born in a stable, and he spent his whole life living among the poor, the oppressed, the hungry, the outcast, people others despised. He then died on the cross for our salvation.

The blessings Jesus gives

When the seventy were sent out by Jesus to heal and to preach, they must have been apprehensive about what would happen and what kind of reception they would receive. Much to their surprise, they witnessed amazing things. They saw demons cast out in the name of Jesus. They could hardly believe their eyes. God was at work, using people like them to demonstrate his power. They were so excited and returned to Jesus full of joy (Luke 10:17).

As we look back over our lives, we are not sure what we have achieved. We are aware of moments of failure, opportunities missed, and broken relationships. There are things we have said and done which we regret. We have sometimes given a talk or preached a sermon, and wondered afterwards whether anyone found it helpful at all. But just occasionally when we have spoken, we have been aware of the presence of God being with us and that the Word of God was ministering to people's hearts. We have often talked about the need for more workers in the harvest field, but wondered whether anyone was listening. Yet, once or twice during our ministry, someone has told us, often many years after the event, that a certain talk had been used by God to call them into ministry.

One precious memory was the time we were in Nairobi and visited an Ethiopian congregation. As we approached the church building, a middle-aged balding man came forward and greeted us most warmly, kissing us both in a traditional Ethiopian way. "How good to see you again," he said. "I still have your photograph in my house." We did not recognise him and spent the service trying to work out who he was and where we had met him. After the service he explained that, when he was a twelfth-grader, he had attended a series of talks on 1 Corinthians that I had given for young people in the underground fellowship in Mek'ele over fifteen years before. He said he had found them so helpful and they had had a profound impact on his life. He apologised that he had gone bald prematurely and said he was not as old as he looked! Later he became the general secretary of the Evangelical Churches Fellowship of Ethiopia.

We were so encouraged, just as the seventy were encouraged by what happened when they went out to witness around Galilee. Jesus rejoices that, even though they are immature evangelists, they have had the privilege of seeing God at work. He is glad they are excited, but he does not want them to get carried away by what has happened. They have had the privilege of being used by God but that is not what matters eternally. What is more important is not that they have been able to perform signs and wonders, but that their names have been written in heaven. He tells them, "Do not rejoice that the spirits submit to you, but rejoice that your names are written in heaven" (Luke 10:20). What is important is not what they have done for God, but what God has done for them.

God calls each of us to know him and to serve him, and he has given to each of us gifts and abilities. We may be very aware of our weaknesses and limitations, yet each of us can be grateful to God and the Lord Jesus Christ for saving us and allowing us to spend our lives in his service. Each of us is to play our part in the extension of God's kingdom. Whether it is in our home town, or in our own country, or in some remote corner of the world, we are called to know Jesus and to be a witness for him.

Endnotes

Chapter 1
1. Muriel Wray, *John and Jeeva of India* (Edinburgh House Press, 1946).
2. A collective community in Israel that was traditionally based on agriculture.

Chapter 3
1. Roland Allen, *Missionary Methods: St Paul's or Ours?* (Grand Rapids, MI: Eerdmans, 1962).

Chapter 5
1. Pinchas Lapide, *The Resurrection of Jesus: A Jewish Perspective* (Minneapolis, MN: Augsburg, 1983).
2. Michelle Guinness, *Child of the Covenant* (London: Hodder, 2005).
3. David Harley, *Thailand Report No.7 Christian Witness to the Jewish People* (Wheaton, IL: Lausanne Committee for World Evangelization, 1980).
4. By this time we had left CMJ and joined the staff of All Nations Christian College (see chapter 6).

Chapter 6
1. This includes every category of teachers from nursery teachers to university lecturers.
2. Described in Chapter 8.
3. "Majority World" is an alternative term for "developing world", "Global South", or "Third World". It describes countries in Africa, Asia, South and Central America, and the Caribbean more geographically accurately and less pejoratively than other terms.

Chapter 7
1. Ruth Tucker, *Guardians of the Great Commission* (Grand Rapids, MI: Zondervan, 1988).
2. Together with his wife, Dr Bill had served for eighteen years in

Guatemala and was executive director of the Missions Commission for the World Evangelical Alliance.

Chapter 8

1. Two companion volumes were published by William Carey. One was the result of my doctoral research into mission training centres around the world: David Harley, *Preparing to Serve: Training for Cross-Cultural Mission* (Pasadena, CA: William Carey, 1995). The other was Robert Ferris (ed.), *Establishing Ministry Training: A Manual for Program Developers* (Pasadena, CA: William Carey, 1995).

2. From *Nigeria Evangelical Missionary Institute*, a publicity leaflet (Jos, Nigeria: Nigeria Evangelical Missions Association, 1990), p. 3.

3. David Harley, *Preparing to Serve: Training for Cross-Cultural Mission* (Pasadena, CA: William Carey, 1995), p. 16.

4. William D. Taylor, *Too Valuable to Lose: Exploring the Causes and Cures of Missionary Attrition* (Pasadena, CA: William Carey, 1987).

Chapter 9

1. David Harley, *By Faith and Failure* (Singapore: Zoie Publishing, 2007).

2. David Harley, *By Word and Wonders* (Singapore: Zoie Publishing, 2010).

Chapter 11

1. The course explores the biblical, historical, cultural, and strategic dimensions of God's redemptive story.

Chapter 12

1. Many ancient manuscripts read "seventy" here, while others read "seventy-two". It is impossible to know with certainty which is the correct reading.

2. David Garrison, *Wind in the House of Islam* (Monument, CO: Wigtake, 2014).

3. Dean Flemming, *Contextualization in the New Testament* (Downers Grove, IL: IVP, 2005).

4. Rosemary used this title to show the seminar was about bridging cultural differences in the UK. In the USA she changed the title to "Bagels and Burgers".

Bibliography

Allen, Roland
Missionary Methods: St Paul's or Ours?
(Grand Rapids, MI: Eerdmans, 1962)

Ferris, Robert (ed.)
Establishing Ministry Training: A Manual for Program Developers
(Pasadena, CA: William Carey, 1995)

Flemming, Dean
Contextualization in the New Testament
(Downers Grove, IL: IVP, 2005)

Garrison, David E.
Wind in the House of Islam
(Monument, CO: Wigtake, 2014)

Guinness, Michelle
Child of the Covenant
(London: Hodder, 2005)

Harley, C. David (ed.)
Thailand Report No.7 Christian Witness to the Jewish People
(Wheaton, IL: Lausanne Committee for World Evangelization, 1980)

Harley, C. David
Preparing to Serve: Training for Cross-Cultural Mission
(Pasadena, CA: William Carey, 1995)

Harley, C. David
Missionary Training: The History of All Nations Christian College and its Predecessors 1911–1981
(Utrecht: Boekencentrum, 2002)

Harley, C. David
By Faith and Failure: When God Takes Hold of Right Steps and Wrong Turns
(Singapore: Zoie Publishing, 2007)

Harley, C. David
By Word and Wonders: When God Leads the Way to Freedom
(Singapore: Zoie Publishing, 2010)

Harley, Rosemary, K. & Martin Goldsmith
Who is My Neighbour? World Faiths – Understanding and Communicating
(Carlisle: Authentic, 2003)

Lapide, Pinchas
The Resurrection of Jesus: A Jewish Perspective
(Minneapolis, MN: Augsburg, 1983)

Nigeria Evangelical Missions Association
Nigeria Evangelical Missionary Institute, publicity leaflet
(Jos, Nigeria: NEMA, 1990)

Taylor, William D.
Too Valuable to Lose: Exploring the Causes and Cures of Missionary Attrition
(Pasadena, CA: William Carey, 1987)

Wray, Muriel
John and Jeeva in India
(Edinburgh House Press, 1946)